LIVES

OF THE

CHIEF FATHERS OF NEW ENGLAND.

The Lord our God be with us, as he was with our fathers: let him not leave us, nor forsake us.

1 Kings 8: 57.

VOL. III.

THE LIFE

OF

JOHN ELIOT.

BY NEHEMIAH ADAMS.

LIBRARY EDITION, 100 COPIES.

BOSTON:
1870.

ADVERTISEMENT

BY THE PUBLISHING COMMITTEE.

THE substance of this book is a Lecture delivered in 1842, before the Young Men's Missionary Association of Boston. On application of the Publishing Committee, the author has consented to enlarge it for publication, as one of the Series of the Lives of the New England Fathers.

SEAL OF THE

MASSACHUSETTS (OR SALEM) COLONY.

TRANSLATION.

Seal of the Governor and Colony of Massachusetts Bay in New England.

LIFE OF JOHN ELIOT.

INTRODUCTORY CHAPTER.

Missionary object of the Pilgrims. Seal of Massachusetts Colony. Reasons with the Pilgrims for leaving Holland. Extract from the Royal Charter of the Plymouth Colony. Charter of the Salem Company. Thoughts on this Continent as a field for Missionary efforts. Account of the landing at Plymouth, and the first meeting with the Indians. First Missionary efforts among them. Manners and habits of the New England Indians. Numbers in the various tribes. Reflections on the Missionary character and efforts of the Pilgrims. The May-flower.

A PROMINENT object with the Pilgrim fathers in coming hither, was, to preach the Gospel to the Indians of this Continent.

Many popular orators and writers represent them, as it were, following and worshiping a goddess of liberty. But it was not for the mere liberty of believing and doing what they pleased that they braved the ocean and the perils of this wilderness. Two great motives influenced them. For the liberty of worshiping God according to their own consciences, they "went out not knowing," as the event proved, "whither they went." But this was not all; they had a missionary object in coming here.

It is an interesting fact that the original seal of the Colony of Massachusetts Bay, who arrived and settled at Salem in 1628, had on it a North American Indian, with these words proceeding from his mouth, "Come over and help us." This device on the seal of their colony published to the world the fact that they regarded themselves as foreign missionaries to North America. This was also the case with their brethren of the Plymouth Colony, who arrived eight years before.

The Pilgrims had fled to Holland, from the persecutions of the English Church. In the account of their residence in Holland we find some records which establish beyond a doubt the fact of their missionary intentions in coming to these shores. Governor Bradford, in his History of Plymouth, speaking of the Pilgrims while yet in Holland, says, "This year, (1617,) Mr. Robinson and his Church begin to think of a remove to America, for several weighty reasons, as (1.) The difficulties in Holland discouraged many from coming to them out of England, and obliged many to return. (2.)

By reason of these difficulties with the licentiousness of the youth, and temptations of the place, many of their children left their parents, some of them becoming soldiers, others taking to foreign voyages, and some to dissoluteness and the danger of their souls, to the great grief of their parents, and fear lest their posterity through these temptations and examples should degenerate, and religion die among them. (3.) From an inward zeal and great hope of laying some foundation or making way for propagating the kingdom of Christ to the remote ends of the earth, though they should be but as stepping stones to others."

They obtained letters patent from the crown authorizing them to settle in North Virginia. The following is an extract from the Royal Charter, and is of the same purport with the third reason assigned by Governor Bradford for their removal to America. The Royal Charter says,—"We have thought it fit, according to our kingly duty—to second and follow God's holy will, by which means we may with boldness go on to the settling of so hopeful a work which tendeth to the reducing and conversion of such savages as remain wandering in desolation and distress, to civil society and Christian religion."

It is well known that the Colonists who received this Charter, and sailed for North Virginia, were driven into the waters of Cape Cod, and thus unintentionally landed and settled at Plymouth.

The Charter of "the Colony of Massachusetts Bay," who settled a few years after at Salem, says, "To win and incite the natives of that country to the knowledge and obedience of the only true God and Saviour of mankind and the Christian faith, is, in our royal intention and the adventurer's free profession, the principal end of the plantation."

The Committee of the "Massachusetts" Company, in their letter dated at Gravesend, and addressed to Mr. Endicott, the leader, and afterward the Governor, of the Massachusetts or Salem Colony, say, "For that the propagating the Gospel is the thing we profess above all in settling this plantation, we have been careful to make plentiful provision of good ministers."*

---

* See Laws of Mass. I., page 77, Sect. 8, 9.

"*Whereas one end in planting these parts was to propagate the true religion unto the Indians*, and that divers of them are become subject unto the English, and have engaged themselves to be ready and willing to understand the law of God: It is therefore ordered that such necessary and wholesome laws which are in force, and may be made from time to time, to reduce them to civility of life, shall be once a year, if the times be safe, made known to them by such fit persons as the general court shall appoint."

It is interesting to think of this Continent as having been the object of missionary zeal and efforts with the pilgrim fathers. The place which this continent occupies on the globe is peculiar and interesting. The numerous nations of the old world are crowded together in one hemisphere, and this continent is the prominent object of the other. It did not seem presumption to the pilgrims to believe that God laid its deep foundations by itself, in the midst of the oceans rolling between it and the rest of the globe, for some purpose as singular as its position. In the writings of ancient poets there are remarkable allusions to this continent, when as yet it was undiscovered. Seneca, a Latin writer, who lived at the beginning of the Christian era, has in his "Medea" this declaration: "The time will come in remote years when the ocean will unloose the present boundaries of nature, and a great country will appear. Another Typhis will discover new worlds, and Thule will no longer be the limit of the earth."* Homer and Horace had sung of Islands west of Africa, the Atlantides, which were "the Elysian fields."

---

* "Venient annis
"Secula seris, quibus Oceanus
Vincula rerum, laxet, et ingens
Pateat tellus, Typhis que novos
Deteget orbes; nec sit terris
Ultima Thule"

Medea, Act. 3., v. 375.

Hanno, the Carthaginian general and great navigator, had sailed from the pillars of Hercules, (the straits of Gibraltar,) westward, thirty days. Some suppose that he must have seen America, or some of the neighboring islands.* Columbus verified the dreams and surmises of the world; the Cabots pursued his sublime discoveries, and they, with their Bristol crews, long accustomed to Icelandic fisheries, found this continent. New adventurers carried home some of the native Indians; and, at length, a new Continent, inhabited by wild men, became the subject of intense interest to the civilized world. Our pious forefathers, while yet in the old world, fancied that they heard the Macedonian cry from the Indians here, and it quickened their flight, as they say, "to follow Christ into a waste howling wilderness."

Having been driven into the waters of Cape Cod, instead of North Virginia, and making a safe harbor on Saturday, the Pilgrims fell on their knees and blessed the God of heaven. The Sabbath came; the Mayflower riding at anchor, and the exploring party in the shallop, kept the first Sabbath of the Lord which, perhaps, had ever been recognized in this region, since God rested from his works.

* "America known to the Ancients." Boston, 1773.

"Monday," says Prince, in his New England Chronology, "the people go ashore to refresh themselves;—the whales play round about them, and the greatest store of fowl they ever saw. But the earth here a company of sand hills, and the water so shallow near the shore, they were forced to wade a bow-shot or two to get to land, which being freezing weather, affecteth them with grievous coughs and colds, which after proves the death of many. When they had marched a mile southward, they see five or six savages whom they follow ten miles till night, but could not overtake them, and lodge in the woods. The next day they come to a place of graves, then to some heaps of sand, when they dig into them, and find several baskets full of Indian corn, and take some, for which they purpose to give the natives full satisfaction as soon as they could meet with any of them." Two days after, they returned to borrow more corn; the ground had frozen a foot deep, but they made up their corn, says Governor Morton, to ten bushels; the next day some of the party, having spent the night there, dug again into some little hillocks, but they found that instead of being cornhills they were graves. By the overruling providence of God, the corn which they had thus borrowed with such good intent to repay, furnished them with seed for the ensuing spring. Here we have the first scene of their approach to the wild objects of their pious and benevolent endeavors.

During the month of February, after their arrival, the colony were afterwards informed that the Indians assembled all their Powwaws, or the conjurers of the country, to curse them with their horrid ceremonies and incantations. They held their assembly for this purpose in a dark and dismal swamp.

On the morning of March 16th, however, they say a savage boldly came alone along the houses straight to the rendezvous, and surprised them with calling out, "Welcome, Englishmen! Welcome, Englishmen!" It seems that he had learned some broken English from the fishermen of Nova Scotia. He said that his name was Samoset, that he was sagamore or lord of a country "a day's sail thence with a great wind," or five days land travel. He told them that four years ago all the inhabitants of the place where they then were, (now Plymouth,) died of an extraordinary plague; that there was neither man, woman, nor child remaining. At night they lodged and watched him. A few days after he returned with an Indian named Squanto, whom a man by the name of Hunt had carried to Spain with nineteen others, and who by some means went to England, and lived in Cornhill, London, with Mr. John Slanie, merchant. He could speak a little English, and thus he was extremely useful to the colonists in assisting them to trade and make treaties with the surrounding Indians. They endeavored to conciliate the natives, but wisely mingled intimations that they were prepared to resist them if attacked.

The treacherous tribe of Narragansett Indians, with five thousand fighting men, who at first made a treaty with the settlers, showed signs on one occasion of hostility. Canonicus, their chief Sachem, sent a bundle of arrows, tied with a snake's skin, which Squanto told them meant a challenge. Governor Bradford and his Council sent them word that if they had rather have war than peace, they might begin when they would; they had done the Indians no wrong, nor did they fear them; nor would the Indians find them unprepared. Then, with some wit, the Governor sent them, by another messenger, the snake's skin filled with powder and bullets; but they refused to receive it, and sent it back.

Thus, after various alarms, and treaties, the pilgrims had fortified themselves in the country, and individuals among them had begun the pious work of instructing some of the young Indians in the Christian religion.

In 1621, one year after the arrival at Plymouth, Elder Robert Cushman sent word to his friends in England that many of the Indians, especially the younger of them, were teachable; that if the Colony had means they would bring up hundreds of them to labor, and learning, and that young men in England who desired to further the Gospel among these poor heathen, would do well to come over and spend their estates, time, and labor, in so doing.

During the few first years after the settlement at Plymouth, several of the natives gave evidence of conversion, and instances of happy death occurred among them. But the hardships and trials incident to a removal into this wilderness delayed the systematic and general efforts of the settlers to convert the Indians. Individuals, however, were laboring among them with success. In 1636, the Plymouth Colony enacted laws to provide for the preaching of the Gospel among the Indians, and ten years after, the Massachusetts Colony passed a similar act.

In 1675, it was ascertained that the whole number of Indians in New England, beginning as far east as the St. Croix River, was about fifty thousand. Of these, about twelve thousand were in the neighborhood of the Massachusetts and the Plymouth Colonies.

At the settlement of this country there were five principal nations, or sachemships, of Indians, in this part of New England, viz. 1. The Pequots; 2. The Narragansetts; 3. The Pawkunnawkuts; 4. The Pawtucketts; 5. The Massachusetts. Each of these nations included several tribes, governed by sagamores.

The Pequots formerly had 4000 warriors; in 1674, 300.

The Narragansetts formerly had 5000 warriors; in 1674, 1000.

The Pawkunnawkuts formerly had 3000 warriors; in 1674, nearly extinct.

The Pawtuckets formerly had 3000 warriors; in 1674, 250.

The Massachusetts formerly had 3000 warriors; in 1674, 300.

The *Pequots* inhabited the most southerly parts of New England, their country for the most part fell under the Connecticut jurisdiction. Their principal sachem lived at or near New London, called, in their language Pequot.

The *Narragansetts* occupied Rhode Island, and other islands in Narragansett bay.

The *Pawkunnawkuts* inhabited the region of the Plymouth Colony, and their sachem held sway over the Sagamores of Nantucket, Martha's Vineyard, and neighboring places. A few years before the arrival of the Pilgrims, a great number of this nation of Indians as before stated, were swept away by a plague, and thus the way was opened for the entrance of the Pilgrims.

The *Pawtuckets* lived to the north, and northeast of the Massachusetts Indians. They were almost wholly destroyed by the plague just mentioned.

The *Massachusetts* Indians dwelt principally about the parts of Massachusetts bay which were first settled by the English, and bordering, some of them, on the region of the Pawkunnawkuts. They were very numerous and powerful. Their chief sachem held rule over many petty chiefs. This people was also visited by the plague in 1612–13, which destroyed the most of them, and prepared the way for the English settlers.

This fact has often brought to mind these words of David: "We have heard with our ears, O God, our fathers have told us what work thou didst in their day, in the times of old. How thou didst drive out the heathen with thy hand, and plantedst them; how thou didst afflict the people and cast them out. For they got not the land in possession by their own sword, neither did their own arm save them; but thy right hand, and thine arm, and the light of thy countenance, because thou hadst a favor unto them."

An early New England writer* says, that he had not been able to learn accurately the nature of the disease or plague which depopulated the Indian tribes in the remarkable manner already described; but that he had "discoursed" with some old Indians, who told him that the patients were "all over exceedingly yellow," and this they described by showing him a yellow garment which the bodies of the victims resembled in color, both before and after death. There is a tradition that a Frenchman, who not long before this plague, had fallen into their hands by shipwreck, told them, as some of the surviving shipmates reported, just before he died by their hands, that "God was angry with them for their wickedness, and would not only destroy them all, but would also people their country with men who would not live after their brutish manners." Those infidels then blasphemously replied, that God could not kill them; which blasphemous mistake was confuted by an horrible and unusual plague, whereby they were

* Mather.

consumed in such vast multitudes, that our first planters found the land almost covered with their unburied carcases, and they that were left alive were smitten into awful and humbler regards of the English by the terrors which the Frenchman's prophecy had imprinted on them.

When the Pilgrims in Holland thought of coming to this country, some of them hesitated for several reasons, and among others through their fear of the savages, who they heard were "cruel, barbarous, and treacherous, being most furious in their rage, and merciless where they overcome, not being content only to kill and take away life, but delight to torment men in most bloody manner that may be, flaying men alive with the shells of fishes, cutting off the points and members of others by piecemeals, and broiling them on the coals, and causing men to eat the collops of their flesh in their sight whilst they live; with other cruelties horrible to be related."* Some were therefore in favor of settling in Guiana, in South America. But they feared the jealousy of the Spaniards, and finally concluded to settle within the jurisdiction of the company of Virginia, where the English, in 1607, had made a settlement. In this way, they supposed that they could also

* Governor Bradford's History of Plymouth.

have better access to the savages, "to reduce them to civil society, and the Christian religion." But God brought them by a way they knew not, having first in part cut off the heathen nations to bring them in.

The May-flower sailed from Holland, September 6, 1620, for the Hudson River. But they were driven into the waters of Cape Cod, and it was a current belief that the shipmaster was bribed by the Dutch to change her course, because the Dutch wished to settle in the region for which the Pilgrims embarked. But some of the best authorities deny this, and say that the change of their course was accidental.

There is so much connection between climate and characters that we may reasonably suppose it to have been the intention of Providence to plant the Pilgrims in this cold region, and on this hard soil, that they might be and do that which is proved to have been their high destiny to be and to accomplish. Whereas, had they settled in a warmer and more enervating latitude, we cannot believe that such a New England as we now behold would have arisen; it would have been easier for the settlers to have borne the imposition of slavery from the mother country, whereas here in Massachusetts the sturdy vigor and independence which were borne and nourished on this rocky and sandy soil, grew impatient of slavery, and soon threw it off, and hence in part the present difference between the North and the South, in some of the essential elements of natural prosperity. God brought the Pilgrims into these bays and harbors, and to this northern soil, because here the qualities necessary to their future usefulness and greatness as a nation could be most successfully developed and strengthened. Instead of reducing the savages to slavery as they might have done had the institution of slavery been fastened upon them in southern regions, they "reduced the savages to civil society, and the Christian religion." Let us return for a moment to the landing of the Pilgrims.

When the May-flower had cast anchor, the Pilgrims fitted up the little shallop which they had brought in their vessel, and coasted the Cape for about a month to determine on the best place for landing and settlement. Having at length fixed on a place, the shallop, with the exploring party came to anchor on Saturday, the 9th of December, corresponding to December 20, New Style. The Sabbath dawned upon them, but the exploring party remained on board, notwithstanding the inmates of the May-flower were still at anchor, waiting to know the result of the exploration. How beautiful and striking was the coincidence of their arriving at Plymouth on the eve of the Sabbath. What a Sabbath it must have been to them. Not only was their comfortless and perilous voyage in a crowded vessel, and their anxious search for a landing place now over, but their persecutions in the old world, their oppressive treatment from the Established Church for not conforming to rites and practices which they could not observe, had now come to an end. Now they had found a new world where they might believe and worship as they pleased. Now they would no longer be taxed for the support of worship in which they had no share. Now their ministers would no longer be ill-used or nick-named, for not conforming to unscriptural practices; now they would not be obliged to keep Lent, and Ash-Wednesday, Candlemas, Christmas, and All-Saints'-day, in a manner repugnant to their consciences. As they looked on this great wilderness, free from all corruptions of man in the worship of God, and pure in that respect as the virgin snows that covered the evergreens, and sheeted the old sand wastes, and shone on the distant hills, they could breathe freely, as they said in the words which indicate the essential spirit of their faith, God is a spirit, and they that worship him, must worship him in spirit and in truth. The world has never seen such a sight, before or since, as that shallop and the May-flower in Plymouth Bay, with the progenitors of this great and glorious New England; fleeing from the old world, arriving at this new world and keeping Sabbath at anchor in these waters. What has ever happened to be likened to it since the time when Noah and his family sailed away from the old world, which had corrupted itself before God, and transplanted the religion of the true God for a new beginning? It would have been interesting to have heard the prayers, and songs of praise, and words of Scripture, with which they kept the Sabbath in their floating Bethels. We notice here that Puritan regard for the Sabbath which has ever characterized New England, and on which her safety so much depends. How natural it would have been for the voyagers to have leaped ashore at the first moment of their arrival in the harbor which they had concluded to make their home. How many passengers now in similar circumstances, would deny themselves the pleasure of exchanging the wearisome confinement on ship-board, for the excitement and satisfaction of exploring their new home? But the Pilgrims would not begin the work of their settlement, of removing any of their effects from the vessel, on the Lord's day, and since the time when God rested from his work on the Sabbath, there has not been a more sublime act of rest and of worship, than was observed by that Pilgrim band.

All this was in accordance with their character and intentions as a missionary band, and for its relation to this view of their character we have dwelt at large upon this incident in their history.

It cannot be impressed too deeply upon our minds that our forefathers did not come here merely to "enjoy their liberty," not merely to flee from persecution, not to increase their worldly estate; they came here, among other good reasons, as they expressly declare, to extend the kingdom of Christ, and the Royal Charter professed that the royal object in granting it was that they might reduce such savages as they found wandering in desolation and distress to civil society and the Christian religion. Does any one cherish a feeling of reverence and love for these pilgrims in view of their sacrifices and efforts to found these institutions which we possess, who yet feels no interest in the work of propagating the gospel to the ends of the earth? Let him consider that a company of Christian missionaries going from this land and settling in India, or Africa, or Oceanica, may be the founders of just such institutions as we enjoy, among the people to whom they are sent. Let every missionary consider that in distant years he may be justly regarded as a pilgrim-father to some portion of the earth for whom he may have done as much as the New England Pilgrims have done for New England. The object of Christian missions is to re-produce and multiply our Christian institutions in heathen and pagan lands. The opportunity of laying foundations in heathen wilds, similar to those which the Pilgrims laid here, has not come to an end. Many a missionary bark may yet be, essentially, a May-flower to distant parts of the earth. Some islands which were filled with savages as barbarous as our Indians, have had their independence recognized by Christian nations, and have taken their place among the nations of the earth; and that band of American missionaries who left these shores for the Sandwich Islands in 1820, and who went round Cape Horn singing the old hymn in the tune of Melton Mowbray,

> "Head of the church triumphant,
> We cheerfully adore thee," &c.,

and who planted the Gospel on those islands, will no doubt in after times have their names enshrined by a grateful posterity in those distant seas. The little schooner which the Rev. John Williams, the martyr of Rarotonga, built with his own hand, to visit the islands of the Harvey group, was a real "May-flower." Prophetic visions of the effects of the Gospel we see fulfilled on these shores and around the globe. Here, emphatically, "instead of the thorn has come up the fir-tree, and instead of the brier the myrtle-tree." In what way can we cherish the memory of our Pilgrim fathers better than to keep alive in us and our children that zeal to spread the Christian religion and Christian institutions, which was one of the strong impulses that bore them across the flood? As the missionary spirit was the native air in which the pilgrim faith was born and nurtured, we may believe that the same spirit will most effectually cherish those institutions and laws which are the fruit of their wisdom. That spirit is a sincere desire to see the glory of God promoted in the world, a willingness to make efforts and sacrifices "that his way may be known on earth, his saving health among all nations."

"The May-flower"! That name must have been proposed by some gentle wife, or by some sweet child, to the man who built that favored vessel! She was, in her seasonableness, more than a *May-flower;* she was the Crocus among the eternal snows and the dreary winter of this western savage world. In the selection of her for the great mission which she accomplished, angels might have said to her, as they came to be ministering spirits to those in her who were to be, in more than one sense, "heirs of salvation," as Gabriel said to Mary, "Hail, thou that art highly favored—the Lord is with thee!" The name of this vessel is one of those instances, of which we see so many in the word, the providence of God, in which "the beauty of the Lord our God" appears in connection with his acts of renown. To the cold eye of reason that name was only a mercantile accident; the eye of faith is willing to be accounted visionary while it sees in it that same hand which, after the deluge, selected the rainbow instead of a periodical tempest, or a Dead Sea, as the memorial of a covenant with the earth.

The painting of the Landing of the Pilgrims, by Weir, justly represents some of the pilgrim company as of cultivated and even polished appearance and manners; they were not the offscouring of the earth. They were men and women of whom, in their day, the world was not worthy. For scholarship, intelligence, and moral worth, the Pilgrims and their associates in the old countries would have been ornaments to the land which chased them away. The reader will find this illustrated in a satisfactory manner in the Life of the Rev. John Cotton, by the Rev. A. W. M'Clure, in the first two volumes in this series of the Lives of eminent N. E. Puritans.

CHAPTER II.

Description of the Indians. Their manners, habits, mode of life, &c. Efforts to convert them, previous to Eliot's labors.

Some account of the manners and habits of the Indians, as our forefathers and their successors found them, will be necessary that we may appreciate the labors and self-denial which were required of those who instructed these sons of the forest in religion and civilization. A correct knowledge of their original condition dispels the romantic associations which many have with the name of a North American Indian. The lowest degradation had been reached by these savages. The laws of a people are a true picture of the people, and some of the laws which the Indians enacted when they began to be civilized, reveal the misery and filthiness from which they began at last to be recovered. This will be illustrated as we proceed.

We will speak first of the personal appearance of the Indian.

Their skin was of a tawny color, a yellowish, dark complexion. Their form and limbs were well proportioned, and it was seldom that a crooked person was found among them. Their hair was long, black, and coarse, without curling; their eyes black, without lustre. In their general appearance they were so much like the Moors of Africa, that many have supposed them to have come originally from that part of the world.

They had many wives, but one of them was chief in her husband's regard. They put away their wives, and the wife also left her husband when offended with him.

Their revengeful disposition is proverbial. The relatives of an injured or murdered Indian regarded his wrong as done to them, and they sought satisfaction in the death of the offender, or in the payment of wampum, (or shells,) which passed with them for money.

They were an idle race, especially the men. Tillage was chiefly performed by the women, though to but little extent. The women also carried burdens, as in removing from place to place. They also prepared the food.

Their wigwams were made with slim poles fixed in the ground, bent, and fastened at the top with the bark of trees. The best of them were made tight and warm with the whole barks of trees, pressed when green by a heavy weight of timber. A common sort of bulrushes woven together, made mats for the covering of the poorer houses. The houses varied in size, from twenty to forty feet square, and some were from sixty to a hundred feet long, and thirty feet broad. In the smaller houses a fire was kindled in the centre, but in the larger, several fires were made for the convenience of the inmates. A hole in the top of the house served the place of a chimney, and on the top of the house a mat was suspended, to serve the purpose of a ventilator to the smoke, being set to the windward side. Their bedsteads were made of rude boards split from the tree, and raised about a foot from the ground, covered with skins, or with mats of woven grass, or bulrushes.

Their principal food was a kind of pottage in which it would be difficult to say what article prevailed. Indian corn, kidney beans, all kinds of flesh and fish, cut in small pieces with the bones, many kinds of roots, artichokes, groundnuts, squashes, oak acorns, walnuts, and chestnuts, were boiled together. The nuts being dried, and powdered, were used as flour to thicken the mess. They made a cake of parched corn, which they called nokake. This they took with them in their travels, and is said to have been so hearty a kind of food, that they subsisted on it many days in their wanderings from place to place.

Their household utensils corresponded in simplicity to their food, and mode of cooking. The pots were made of clay, in the shape of an egg without the top. They were glad to receive pots of metal, as the earth of which they made their brittle vessels was scarce and dear. They used a kind of wood which was not liable to split, for dishes, spoons, and ladles. Their water pails were made of birch bark, folded square, with a handle or bail. Some of them held two or three gallons, and they could make one of them in the space of an hour. They wrought pictures of birds, beasts, fishes and flowers of divers colors in their baskets, which were made of corn husks, silk grass, and wild hemp.

They formerly used no drink but water, though they soon learned from the settlers the manufacture and use of cider. When they became acquainted with intoxicating drinks, they showed a violent love for them, by which their savage passions and propensities were fearfully excited.

Their clothing was, at first, of skins, and some had mantles of birds' feathers, twilled together. Even the most barbarous of them were decent in covering their persons, and were never seen naked in public.

One of their principal remedies in sickness was, to put the patient, and sometimes several patients together, in a rude stone house, which they would heat by building fires round it, and having thus put the sick into a violent perspiration, they would plunge them into a neighboring brook.

They divided time into sleeps, and moons, and winters. It is a curious fact that they called the Constellation, Charles' Wain, by the same name with the English, the Bear. Like the early eastern nations, they seem to have pondered the face of the heavens, and to have made figures of the stars.

Their money consisted of shells, or strings of shells, the black being double in value to the white. The *mints* of their money seem to have been at Block Island, and Long Island, upon whose sandy flats and shores, these welk shells were chiefly found. It was called wompompeague, or, wompeague, and by contraction, wompum, or, wampum. They redeemed captives, paid tribute, made satisfaction for wrongs, and murders, and purchased peace of their more powerful neighbors, with strings of this wampum.

Their weapons were bows and arrows, clubs, tomahawks, made of wood like a pole axe, with a sharp stone in the head. They used targets or shields of bark.

They formerly smeared their skin with bears' grease, but when the English swine afforded them lard, they used it as a substitute, and thus having anointed themselves, they painted their faces with vermilion, or red, and powdered their heads. Sometimes they painted one half of the face black, and the other white, and so, with various colors, deformed their visages, the women, especially, doing this, and the warriors thereby making themselves hideous in battle. Widows, mourning for their husbands, painted their faces wholly black. The men preparing for war put their hair in a roll, and surmounted it with turkey's or eagle's feathers, with other fantastic and showy decorations.

They took great pleasure in dancing, the men only dancing, and they singly, (except in the war dance,) with uncouth and antic gestures and movements of the whole body, the spectators singing or whooping. The dancer took off his ornaments one by one as he danced, and gave them away to those who looked on, and when he had given away all that he had upon him, and was weary, another would succeed him, and thus succeeding each other they would spend the nights of a whole week together, sleeping by day. At such dancings accompanied with revelings, chiefly held after harvest, they were addicted to many evil practices.

They were a hospitable race. Strangers were furnished with the best food and lodging, and were served before themselves.

Their government was for the most part monarchical, the chief sachem or sagamore making his will the law, though there were chief men associated with him as counselors. In some of the tribes the influence of the head men was greater than in others, making the government a mixture of monarchy and aristocracy.

They had no idols made with hands, but being ignorant of the true God, they adored natural objects; the sun, the moon, the earth, fire, and other things. They supposed that every thing in nature has a god in it, or belonging to it, but fire they believed to be itself a god. They believed that there was one god in the southwest, who was the chief deity.

The Indians had priests or powows, or, powaws, who were conjurers, who, with horrid rites and incantations, told their fortunes, advised them in their affairs, yelled over them in their sick and dying moments, and performed religious worship with terrific noises and actions,

> " Like stabled wolves or tigers at their prey,
> Doing abhorred rites to Hecate."

The Indians believed in the immortality of the soul, that the good are admitted to a splendid entertainment, and the wicked wander in agony forever, and that there is no resurrection of the body for good or bad.

As to the origin of the Indians, Roger Williams has well expressed the truth on the subject, in his Key into the language of the Indians of New England.*

"From Adam and Noah that they spring, it is granted on all hands. But for their later descent, and whence they came into these parts, it seems hard to find, as to find the well-head of some fresh stream which running many miles out of the country to the salt ocean, hath met with many mixing streams by the way."

Mr. Williams gives many particulars of their manners and customs; some of which are here added.

Their nokake, or nokehick, parched meal, was carried by each man on a journey, or in war, in a basket, fastened to his back, or in a hollow

* Mass. Hist. Soc., Coll. 1794., p. 205.

belt. With a spoonful of this meal, and a spoonful of water from the brook, Mr. Williams says he has many a time made a good supper. This parched meal, boiled with water, he says, is the wholesomest diet they have. *Nawsaump* was a kind of meal pottage unparched, and from this the English derived their *samp*, or Indian corn, broken and boiled, and eaten, hot or cold, with milk or butter; "which are mercies beyond the natives' plain water, and which is a dish exceeding wholesome for the English bodies."

Tobacco was in general use among them, and was the only plant which the men cultivated, the women attending to the rest. The following remark, by Mr. Williams, is in good illustration of former views and feelings with regard to the use of spirituous liquors. "I never see any take tobacco so excessively as I have seen men in Europe; and yet excess were more tolerable in them, because they want the refreshing of beer and wine, which God had vouchsafed Europe." *

They made up a fire, when they were lying down to sleep, summer and winter. "Their fire," says Williams, "is instead of our bed clothes. And so themselves, and any that

* Key, p. 213.

have occasion to lodge with them, must be content to turn often to the fire, if the night be cold; and they who first wake must repair the fire."

Bad dreams they considered as threatenings from God; and when they happened to them, they would engage in prayer at all times of the night. An Indian once dreamed that the sun, whom they worship as a god, darted a beam into his breast. This he took for an admonition ot his death. He called his friends and neighbors together, and prepared some refreshment for them; but himself remained awake, and fasting, for ten days and nights in great humiliation and distress.

"The women nurse all the children themselves; yet a rich or high woman maintains a nurse to tend the child."

"They have amongst them natural fools, either so born, or accidentally deprived of reason."

"The toothache is the only pain which will force their stout hearts to cry. I have never heard any cries among them like those of men in the toothache. In this pain they use a certain root dried, not much unlike our ginger."

"They are most skillful in cutting off the heads of their enemies in fight. I know the man, yet living, who pretended to fall from his own camp to the enemy, proffered his service in the front with them against his own army. He drew them out to battle, keeping in front; but, on a sudden, shot their chief leader and captain, and, in a trice, fetched off his head, and returned immediately to his own again. His act was false and treacherous; yet herein appear policy, stoutness, and activity."

"Their desire of and delight in news, is great as the Athenians. A stranger that can relate news in their own language they will style him manittoo, a god."

In hearing news they sit in a circle, two, three, or four deep. "I have seen near a thousand in a round where English could not well near half so many have sitten."

They frequently inquired "Why came the Englishmen hither?" The explanation most commonly believed among themselves at first was, that the English wanted fire-wood, and so removed to these parts, as the Indians remove when they have used up the wood around them.

They kept the time of the day and the night with great accuracy, by observing the sun, moon, and stars. Living abroad in the fields and sleeping much out of doors, even the young children were expert in telling the time. The Indians were punctual in their promises as to time. Mr. Williams says they once charged him with lying for not being punctual, though necessarily delayed.

English travelers were struck with the paths which the bare and tough feet of the Indians had made in stony places. One writer says that he has known many of them to run between eighty and a hundred miles in a summer's day, and return within two days. He says they were so thoroughly acquainted with the interior of the country by means of hunting, that they have guided travelers forty miles without any path. They coveted horses above other beasts, preferring the ease of riding even to the comfort of milk and butter from the cow. On meeting with one another in travel, they were very happy and joyful; and striking fire, with stones or sticks, took tobacco, and set down to talk. It was quite rare to meet an old man or a lame man with a staff, their constitutions being generally robust.

The English settlers were greatly struck with the purity of the air and of the water in New England.* But as New England is about twelve degrees south of England, the greater cold of this region is explained, Mr. Williams thinks, by the fact that main lands and conti-

* See Appendix, B.

nents are colder than islands. "England's winds are sea winds, which are commonly more thick and vapory, and warmer winds. The northwest wind, which occasioneth New England cold, comes over the cold, frozen land, and over many millions of loads of snow. And yet the pure wholesomeness of the land is wonderful, and the warmth of the sun such in the sharpest weather, that I have often seen the natives' children run about stark naked in the coldest days, and the Indian men and women lie by a fire in the woods in the coldest nights; and I have often been out myself such nights without fire, mercifully and wonderfully preserved."

It is observed by many writers that the Indians had a considerable mixture of sadness in their disposition. Though nature here was profuse in wild animals for food, and fish, and fowl, and fruits, the savages were subject to much suffering from causes which they had no knowledge to understand nor skill to prevent. Their superstitions joined with their savage vices made them afraid. It would seem also, in noticing the proofs of this disposition to melancholy, that the coming event of their disappearance as a race had cast its shadow upon their spirits. Mr. Williams says that they dislike cloths inclining to white, "but preferred to have a sad color, without any whitish hairs, suiting with their own natural temper, which inclines to sadness."*

In the spirit with which our forefathers came hither, seeking the conversion of the red race, good men from time to time pursued different measures for their spiritual good. But while other men deserve great praise for their zeal and industry in this benevolent work, it was reserved to JOHN ELIOT to gain for himself the name of the Apostle to the Indians. The way in which he obtained it will now appear, and also some account of his life and character, with further notices respecting the Indians.

Though individuals had incidentally labored among the Indians for their spiritual good before the Apostle Eliot began his efforts to give them the Gospel, and some useful impressions had been made on some of their minds, the first systematic efforts for their conversion were made by him. Roger Williams' narrative was printed in London, in 1643. Eliot began to preach in the Indian tongue in 1646. Mr. Williams says,

"Many solemn discourses I have had with all sorts of nations of them, from one end of the country to the other, so far as opportunity, and the little language I have, could reach.

* See Appendix, C.

"I know there is no small preparation in the hearts of multitudes of them. I know their many solemn confessions to myself, and one to another, of their last wandering conditions.

"I know not with how little knowledge and grace of Christ the Lord may save; and therefore neither will despair, nor report much.

"Two days before the death of Wequash, the Pequot captain, as I passed up to Quunnihticut (Connecticut) river, it pleased my worthy friend, Mr. Fenwick, whom I visited at his house in Saybrook fort, at the mouth of that river, to tell me that my old friend Wequash lay very sick. I desired to see him, and himself was pleased to be my guide two miles where Wequash lay.

"Amongst other discourses concerning his sickness and death, in which he freely bequeathed his son to Mr. Fenwick, I closed with him concerning his soul. He told me that some two or three years before, he had lodged at my house, where I acquainted him with the condition of all mankind, and his own in particular; how God created man and all things; how man fell from God, and his present enmity against God and the wrath of God against him till repentance. Said he, your words were never out of my heart to this present; and, said he, 'Me much pray to Jesus Christ.' I told him so did many English, French, and Dutch, who had never turned to God nor loved him. He replied in broken English: 'Me so big naughty heart: me heart all one stone!' Savoring expressions using to breathe from compunct and broken hearts, and a sense of inward hardness and unbrokenness. I had many discourses with him in this life; but this was the sum of our last parting, until our general meeting." *

We now come to the history of the man by whom the work of converting and civilizing the Indians was carried out with the most signal success.

---

* Roger Williams' Key, p. 26.

CHAPTER III.

John Eliot. Birth and Education. Associated with Rev. Thomas Hooker. Arrives at Boston. Settles in Roxbury. Anecdote. Discovery of Spot Pond. Marriage. Christian and Ministerial character. His zeal for common School Education. Notices of his personal character. His Congregational Sentiments. Remarks upon them. Mr. Eliot's children. His prayers. His preaching. Infant Baptism.

JOHN ELIOT was born in Nasing, Essex, England, in the year 1604. All that is known of his parents is, that they were eminently pious, to which Mr. Eliot bore testimony, when he wrote in after life these words: "I do see that it was a great favor of God unto me to season my first years with the fear of God, the word, and prayer."

He was educated in England at the University of Cambridge, and was distinguished for his love of the languages, in which he attained uncommon skill, especially in Hebrew and Greek. There is a connection between this fact and his labors in New England in acquiring the Indian tongue and translating the Bible and other books into it.

The Rev. Thomas Hooker, afterwards the

first Pastor of the Church in Cambridge, New England, who afterwards removed with his Church to Hartford, Connecticut, had been silenced for his conscientious scruples at certain rites and observances in the Church of England, after exercising the ministry four years. At the suggestion and request of distinguished individuals, he established a school in the town of Little Braddow, near Chelmsford, in the county of Essex, England. Mr. Eliot was an usher in this school. In this school several individuals were trained up who became eminently useful. Mr. Eliot wrote an account of this school; and says of it, and of his connection with the family of Mr. Hooker, "To this place was I called through the infinite riches of God's mercy in Christ Jesus to my poor soul; for here the Lord said unto my dead soul, Live; and, through the grace of Christ, I do live, and I shall live forever. When I came to this blessed family, I then saw, and never before, the power of godliness in its lively vigor and efficacy."

By the influence of Mr. Hooker, Mr. Eliot was led to devote himself to the Christian ministry. Seeing the corruptions of the Church of England, and the oppressive spirit of those in authority towards all who would not conform to the ceremonies and practices of the Established

Church, he resolved that he would go to America, that he might preach the gospel without restraint.

He came to Boston in November, 1631, in the ship "Lyon," with Governor Winthrop's lady and children, and sixty others. There was then no minister at the Church in Boston, Rev. Mr. Wilson, their pastor, having gone to England to settle his affairs. Mr. Eliot joined the Church at Boston, and preached to them a part of a year, till the return of Mr. Wilson, when the Church wished to make him colleague and teacher with Mr. Wilson. But he had engaged with several individuals, in England, that if they should remove to America, he would be their minister. They came the year after his arrival, and settled at Roxbury; and having formed a Church there, secured the services of Mr. Eliot. He was then twenty-eight years old, and he continued as Pastor of the Church in Roxbury nearly sixty years. His meeting-house was on the hill where the present meeting-house of the First Church in Roxbury (unitarian) now stands. Cotton Mather has preserved an anecdote connected with this hill, illustrating the art which Mr. Eliot had at spiritualizing. Going up the hill to his meeting-house, in his old age, with much feebleness and weariness he said to the one who led him, "This is very like the way to heaven, 'tis up hill; the Lord by his grace fetch us up." Spying a bush near him he instantly added, "And truly there are thorns and briars in the way too!" which instance, Mather says, "I would not have singled out from the many thousands of his occasional reflections, but only that I might suggest unto the good people of Roxbury something for them to think upon when they are going up to the house of the Lord." *

In February of the year after his arrival, Mr. Eliot is mentioned as one of the company who, with the governor, made an excursion into the vicinity of Boston, and discovered a pond to which they gave its present name of "Spot Pond."† This pond has of late been a prominent candidate for the privilege of supplying this city with water.

In 1632, Mr. Eliot was married to the pious young lady to whom he was betrothed in England, and who came to America by appointment the year after Mr. Eliot's arrival. We shall have occasion to speak of her in the sequel of this history.

In the exercise of the Christian ministry, Mr.

* Mag. B. III. Life of Eliot. Art. 1.

† Sparks' Lib. Am. Biog. V. 9. Francis' Life of Eliot.

Eliot was remarkable for a deep sense of the great responsibleness of his work. It made him humble; he seemed to have a peculiar fear of the temptations incident to his profession, and to be deeply impressed with the weight of its duties. His brethren in the ministry were struck with this characteristic of his ministerial deportment.

He bestowed much labor and diligence upon his preparations for the pulpit. It is said that when he listened to a discourse which seemed to have had care and attention bestowed upon it, he was accustomed to express his approbation and thanks to the preacher. But while his discourses showed him to be a student, he placed a higher value on spiritual gifts in preaching than upon the greatest accomplishments of art or labor. He frequently exhorted young preachers to make Christ prominent in their discourses and in all their ministrations.

He had an elevated sense of the meaning and privilege of church-membership. With affection, but also with plain and faithful words, he never ceased to rebuke the inconsistencies of professors of religion. Mather says of him, "He would sound the trumpet of God against all vice with a most penetrating liveliness, and make his pulpit another Mount Sinai, for the flashes of lightning therein displayed against the breaches of the law given from that burning mountain. There was usually a special fervor in the rebukes which he bestowed on carnality. When he was to brand the earthly mindedness of Church members and the allowance and indulgence which they often give themselves in sensual delights, he was a right Boanerges. He spoke as many thunderbolts as words!"

He paid particular attention to the young people of his charge, gave them instruction in public and private with the help of catechisms composed by him especially for their use. It was his familiar habit, when he visited a family, to call the young around him and lay his hands on their heads with words of kindness and prayer.

He showed his love of learning in his zeal for the establishment of common schools. The grammar School at Roxbury owed much to his care. At the meeting of a Synod in Boston, he made the schools of the country a special subject of prayer, beseeching God that he would cause them to be established everywhere, that schools might flourish, that every member of the Synod might go home to procure and encourage a good school in his town; and that before they should die, they might be so happy as to see a good school established in every part of the country.

"God so blessed his endeavors that Roxbury

could not live quietly without a free school in the town, and the issue of it has been one thing that has almost made me put the title of Schola Illustris upon that little nursery; that is, that Roxbury has afforded more scholars first for the College and then for the public than any town of its bigness, or, if I mistake not, of twice its bigness in all New England. From the spring of the school at Roxbury, there have run a large number of the streams which have made glad the whole city of God. I persuade myself that the good people of Roxbury will forever scorn to begrudge the cost, or to permit the death of a school which God has made such an honor to them; and thus the rather because their deceased Eliot has left them a fair part of his own estate for the maintaining of the school in Roxbury; and I hope, or at least I wish that the ministers of New England may be as ungainsayably importunate with their people as Mr. Eliot was with his for schools which may seasonably tinge the young souls of the rising generation. A want of education for them is the blackest and saddest of all the bad omens that are upon us."*

One result of his interest in schools was that many individuals were raised up under his eye

* Mag. Book III., 499.

who became ministers of the gospel, and some of them were eminently useful.

He was so engrossed in the affairs of his ministry that he hardly paid sufficient attention to his worldly affairs, never being anxious about his support, depending wholly on the temporary and voluntary offerings of his people, which varied with the times. Dr. Dwight, in his Travels in New England and New York,* relates an anecdote to illustrate his generous and somewhat improvident disposition and habits. "The parish treasurer having paid him his salary, put it into a handkerchief, and tied it into as many hard knots as he could make to prevent him from giving it away before he reached his own house. On his way he called on a poor family, and told them that he had brought them some relief. He then began to untie the knots, but finding it a work of great difficulty, he gave it to the mistress of the house, saying, "Here, my dear, take it, I believe the Lord designs it all for you."

Like many other ministers, he owed much to the care which his wife took of him and his worldly affairs. She of course did not commend him for such reckless acts of charity as the one just named. One day some cattle stood before

* Vol. III., p. 15.

their door. His wife, to try him, asked him to whom they belonged, and though they were his own, he did not know them.

His influence upon his brethren in the ministry seems to have been eminently spiritual. He once said in a company of them, "The Lord Jesus takes much notice of what is said and done among his ministers when they are together. Let us pray before we depart." His advice to some who complained of the conduct of Church members towards them, was, "Bear, forbear, forgive." On one occasion he came into a meeting of ministers who had met as referees on some difficulties between two parties. A large bundle of papers lay on the table, containing the correspondence and other documents relating to the quarrel. He put them all into the fire, and said, "You need not be astonished at what I have done, for I did it on my knees before I came here."

He loved to attend upon the ministry of his brethren when they lectured during the week. It used to excite surprise, that, with his many labors and studies, he could find so much time to do this. His appearance in the house of God as a hearer was noticeable, being always wakeful and watchful, turning the pages of a Bible to find the texts referred to by the preacher, and on returning to his home, he would preach the sermon over again to those who walked with him.

He is mentioned as remarkable for the value which he seemed to set on the Sabbath, and for the high spiritual enjoyment which its return brought with it. Of every Sabbath it might almost be said with regard to his enjoyment of the sacred hours, " That Sabbath was a high-day."

He was eminently a man of prayer, setting apart whole days for special supplication and communion with God, to which he frequently added fasting. When he had any special difficulty in his private, or in public affairs, he devoted himself to special, secret prayer for some time together, on the principle related of another, " That when we would have any great things to be accomplished, the best policy is to work by an engine which the world sees nothing of." When he heard any special news he would sometimes say, " Brethren, let us turn all this into prayer." When he paid a visit to a family with which he was familiar, he would sometimes say, " Come, let us not have a visit without a prayer; let us pray down the blessing of heaven on your family before we go."

A pious woman, afflicted with a wicked husband, complained to him that she was greatly troubled by the bad company which her husband brought with him into the house, and asked him what she should do. He said to her, "Take the holy Bible into your hands when they come, and you will soon drive them away." The experiment is said to have been successful.

One day walking in his garden with a friend, he began to pluck up the weeds. His friend pleasantly said to him, "Sir, you tell us we must be heavenly-minded," as though he would draw from Mr. Eliot some remarks on the consistency of heavenly-mindedness with attention to things about us. Mr. Eliot replied, "It is true; and this is no impediment unto that; for were I sure to go to heaven tomorrow, I would do what I do to-day."

He went into a merchant's counting room, where he saw his mercantile books on the table, and some books of devotion on the shelf. Upon which he said, "Sir, here is earth on the table, and Heaven on the shelf. Pray don't sit so much at the table as altogether to forget the shelf."

Preaching once on holiness in all manner of conversation, he said, "In the morning if we ask, Where am I to be to-day? our souls must answer, In heaven. In the evening if we ask, Where have I been to-day, our souls may answer,

In heaven. If thou art a believer thou art no stranger to Heaven while thou livest; and when thou diest, Heaven will be no strange place to thee: no, thou hast been there a thousand times before."

He would say to students, "I pray look to it that you be morning birds."

A few years before his death, he pressed his people to obtain another pastor, and said, "'Tis possible you may think the burden of maintaining two ministers may be two heavy for you; but I deliver you from that fear; I do here give back my salary to the Lord Jesus Christ, and now, brethren, you may fix that upon any man that God shall make a pastor for you." But his Church kindly and generously told him that they should count his very presence worth a salary, when he should be so superannuated as to do no further service for them.

He was an abstemious man, and yet far from being morose or censorious, but when invited to a large dinner, it is said that while he eat but very little he would indulge in pleasant and grateful remarks with respect to the plenty with which God had furnished his people in this wilderness. Having been invited at a stranger's house to take some drink, which he was told was wine and water, he replied, "Wine! 'tis a noble, generous liquor, and we should be humbly thankful for it; but, as I remember, water was made before it," and water was his drink, to a degree which was far from being common even in those days.

He was greatly displeased with the increasing attention in his day among the men to the wearing of the hair, the length of it growing to effeminacy, and false hair frequently being added, when there was no necessity for it to cover the head. He finally despaired of changing or checking the custom, and said, "The lust is become insuperable."

It is said of him that no man ever had fewer enemies than he, but still there were those who privately disliked him, and he charged his wife in her visits among the people to do good in a special manner to any whom she found disposed to speak against him, or to entertain unkind feelings towards him. Having once displeased a hearer by something in a sermon, the man abused him publicly by words and by printing something to his injury. The man soon after was wounded. Mrs. Eliot had considerable skill in medicine and the treatment of wounds, and Mr. Eliot sent her to cure the man, which she did, and upon his recovery the man called to thank her, but she took no reward, and Mr.

Eliot kept him to dine, and took no notice of his evil conduct, whereupon the man was deeply affected and subdued.

He had much tact and wit in suiting his benedictions to the conditions and circumstances of different people.

In the days of affliction he showed exemplary resignation to the will of God. He followed to the grave two or three of his sons, who were ministers of the Gospel. But his patience and submission under these trials are spoken of with great commendation.

His love for the Hebrew tongue is seen in the following enthusiastic words: "O that the Lord would put it into the heart of some of his religious and learned servants to take such pains about the Hebrew language as to fit it for universal use! Considering that above all languages spoken by the lip of man, it is most capable to be enlarged, and fitted to express all things, and motions, and notions that our human intellect is capable of in this mortal life, considering also that it is the invention of God himself; and what one is fitter to be the universal language, than that which it pleased our Lord Jesus to make use of when he spake from heaven unto Paul!"

In the government of his family, it is said

that there might have been seen a perpetual mixture of a Spartan and a Christian discipline, and that whatever decay there might have been in family religion generally, the people 'knew how that he would command his children and his household after him, that they should keep the way of the Lord.'

He was remarkable for the efforts he employed to instruct the children, making catechisms for them having reference to any prevailing errors. The effect of this is certified in a remark of Cotton Mather, that it is a well-principled people that he has left behind him. "As when certain Jesuits were sent among the Waldenses to corrupt their children, they returned with much disappointment and confusion, because the children of seven years old were well-principled enough to encounter the most learned of them all; so, if any seducers were let loose to wolve it among the good people of Roxbury, I am confident they would find as little prey in that well instructed place as in any part of the country. No civil penalties would signify so much to save any people from the snares of busy heretics, as the unwearied catechising of our Eliot has done to preserve his people from the gangrene of ill opinion."*

*Book III. Art. IV.

It is said of Mr. Eliot that he was not only an evangelical minister, but a Protestant and a Puritan. "He was a modest, humble, but very reasonable non-conformist unto the ceremonies which have been such unhappy apples of strife in the Church of England; otherwise the dismal thickets of America had never seen such a person in them."

Mr. Eliot was strongly attached to the Congregational form of Church order. He spoke of it as the special gift of Christ to his people who followed him into the wilderness with an earnest zeal for communion with Him in a pure worship. He regarded Congregationalism as a happy medium to "rigid Presbyterianism" on the one hand, and "leveling Brownism" on the other, the liberties of the people not being disregarded, nor the authority of the elders rendered insignificant, but a due balance kept between them both. He regarded the Platform of Church Discipline "as being the nearest of what he had yet seen to the directions of heaven."

By this it is not to be understood that Mr. Eliot as a true Congregationalist, supposed that any form of Church government was imposed by Christ or the Apostles upon the Christian Church, as being in any way essential to the existence of a true Church of Christ. With regard to the appointment of any special form of Church Government, it would seem that there is a wise silence in the New Testament. The genius of Christianity forbids an adherence to any form of ecclesiastical order as essential to the existence of a Church of Christ. This truth was declared by Christ at Jacob's well to the Samaritan woman. The Jews insisted on Jerusalem as the place where men ought to worship. The Samaritans as strenuously maintained that acceptable worship could be performed only in their mountain.

Christ said, The hour cometh when ye shall neither in this mountain nor yet at Jerusalem worship the Father; that is, no place in preference to another shall be essential to acceptable worship. God is a Spirit, and they that worship him need not restrict themselves to any hallowed place, but may worship him any where acceptably, if they worship Him in spirit and in truth.

But if so great a change was allowed as the abolition of sacred places, which once were essential to acceptable worship, and notwithstanding all that had been done to make men feel that Jerusalem and the Temple were the places to which the true worshipers must of necessity resort, it follows that no forms, any more than places, are essential to the true worship of God.

We may infer what form of Church government prevailed under the Apostles, though different readers of the New Testament will draw different inferences. This shows that no form is prescribed as being essential, otherwise we should not have been left in the dark in so important a subject. The body of Moses and the place of his sepulchre were hidden, because as we generally suppose the Israelites would have paid an idolatrous reverence before such a shrine as the tomb of their illustrious leader, and in the Jewish Church the solemn farce of a Holy Sepulchre would have been enacted, in anticipation and in countenance of the subsequent follies which have been connected with the Sepulchre of Christ. We may say of any supposed form of Church government as being in any way essential, as is said of the body of Moses, and for a similar reason, "The Lord buried it," and "no man knoweth of its sepulchre to this day."

Our preference for the Congregational form of Church government is not properly founded on any prescriptions in the New Testament, but on our convictions that this form is most accordant with the genius of Christianity and of republican institutions. But so surely as we insist on Congregationalism as having any "divine right," or authority, and we seek to propagate

Congregationalism with such convictions, we are as surely High Churchmen and Puseyites as can any where be found. To insist on the absence of all forms and on the perfect simplicity of worship, with a sectarian spirit, shows as great an attachment to *a form of worship* as though we urged the adoption of all the ceremonies of the Cathedral. We may be as bigoted in favor of simplicity as of any thing else, and a Quaker and a Congregationalist may be as much a formalist and a Churchman as any other. At the same time we may believe that the Congregational form of government is nearer to the Spirit of the New Testament than any other, and this is what Mr. Eliot probably meant when he said that Congregationalism was nearest in his view to the directions of heaven.

The influence which was exerted upon the mind of Thomas Jefferson, and which he exerted in the framing of the Constitution, by observing, as he did, an illustration of democracy in a Congregational Baptist Church in Virginia, is well known.*

We ought to carry out the true Puritan doctrine of liberty of conscience by not despising any who choose to worship under a different form and order from our own. It is an interesting illustration of the noble spirit in our Puritan

* Jefferson's "Notes on Virginia."

institutions that all sects have liberty here to worship God with any forms or in any manner they please; and he who tries to hinder them any further than by convincing them, or feels sourly towards them in the enjoyment of their liberty of conscience and religious preferences, has not yet learned all that he may of the nature and spirit of religious liberty. But if we profess to be in the true succession from the Puritans and Pilgrims as to doctrine and Church order, let us not mix any of those things with our worship from which the Pilgrims fled to this wilderness, that they might be rid of them. We can live peaceably and freely in the midst of such corruptions and not be persecuted. They could not. Let us not abuse our liberty, by turning again to those beggarly elements of human appointments in Church government and worship which corrupt the religion of Christ. Let us not begin to do so by cultivating the spirit of bigoted attachment to our simple order and forms, for thereby we as truly violate the spirit of Christianity as though we insisted on a multitude of ceremonies and a hierarchy, as essential to a Church. He who says "No Church without simplicity in worship," and he who says, "No Church without a Bishop," are two extremes which meet. At the same time, we shall be the degenerate sons of men who made such sacrifices for purity in worship as did the Pilgrims, unless we adhere to our simple and beautiful mode of Church government and worship as preferable to any other.

The practice of examining persons who seek admission to the Church, was much insisted on by Mr. Eliot. The relation of their experience he says, "is an ordinance of wonderful benefit. The devil knows what he does when he thrusts so hard to get this custom out of our churches. For my part I would say in this case, Get thee behind me Satan; thou givest an horrible offence to the Lord Jesus Christ. Let us keep up this ordinance with all gentleness; and where we see the least spark of grace held forth, let us prize it more than all the wit in the world."

Mr. Eliot had six children, a daughter and five sons. The daughter became exemplary for her piety and matronly deportment. His first son, John, was "a lively, zealous, acute preacher, not only to the English at New Cambridge,*

* Newton. Dr. Homer, in his History of Newton says, "This son of the apostle Eliot was the first minister of Newton. His abilities and occupation in the ministry are said to be pre-eminent. Under the direction of his father, he obtained considerable proficiency in the Indian language, and was an assistant to him in the missionary employment, until he settled at Newton. Even after his ordination there, he imitated the manner of his father, devoting hi -

but also to the Indians thereabout." He died early, and upon his death-bed uttered many remarkable things. The third child, Joseph, was pastor of the Church in Guilford, Conn. The fourth child, Samuel, was a candidate for the ministry, but died young. The fifth was Aaron, who also died very young. The last was Benjamin, who became his father's assistant in the ministry at Roxbury, but died before his father. Of these six children, Mr. Eliot said, "THEY ARE ALL EITHER WITH CHRIST, OR IN CHRIST."

Mather speaks of the singular and surprising successes of Mr. Eliot's prayers; 'for they were such that in our distresses we still repaired to him under that encouragement.' "He is a prophet, and he shall pray for thee, and thou shalt live." He mentions the following fact. They who are displeased at David's imprecations against his enemies, may see in it that a good man may pray for the destruction of the incorrigibly wicked, when great and good ends will be accomplished by it, leaving it submissively to the appointments of the all-wise God. A good man never ventures to pray in this manner, except

self to the instruction of the Indians, as well as his own flock. Accordingly he preached statedly once in a fortnight to them at Pequimet, (Stoughton,) and sometimes at Natick."

when he is under a strong influence, drawing him very near to God with holy freedom and boldness. At such times his feelings are eminently pure; and it is in such times that good men feel impelled to pray for the removal of those who oppose God, and hinder others in their salvation. No doubt if there were more of ardent piety, there would be more of righteous indignation against the obstinate opposers of religion, and we should find ourselves better able to understand the feelings and language of David, when praying against the enemies of his throne and of the God who ruled by him. That language will come into more familiar use by the people of God, in their nearest approaches to him, as they go forth with their King and Saviour in his conflicts with his enemies.

The fact to which the allusion has been made was this:

There was a pious gentleman of Charlestown by the name of Foster, who, with his son, was taken prisoner by the Turks. The news being spread in this vicinity, the good people offered up many prayers for his deliverance. But it was reported that the prince, within whose authority he was a prisoner, had resolved that during his reign, no captive should be set free. The friends and acquaintances of this man then concluded that his captivity was hopeless. Soon after, Mr. Eliot on some public and solemn occasion, used these direct and forcible petitions. "Heavenly Father! work forth deliverance of thy poor servant, Foster; and if the prince which detains him, will not, as they say, dismiss him so long as himself lives, Lord, we pray thee to kill that cruel prince; kill him, and glorify thyself upon him." Soon after the prisoners returned and brought news that in consequence of the untimely death of the prince they had been set at liberty.

There was one thing which seems to have pressed very heavily on the mind and heart of Mr. Eliot in his ministerial office. It was the care of a Church. "He looked upon it," says one, "as a thing no less dangerous than important, and attended with so many difficulties, temptations, and humiliations, as that nothing but a call from the Son of God could have encouraged him unto the susception of it. He saw that it was no easy thing to feed the souls of such a people, to bear their manners with all patience, not being by any of their infirmities discouraged from teaching of them, and from watching and praying over them, to value them highly as the flock of God, which he hath purchased with his own blood, notwithstanding all their miscarriages, and in all to examine the rule of Scripture for the warrant of whatever shall be done, and to remember the day of judgment wherein an account must be given of whatever shall be done, having in the meantime no expectation of the riches and grandeurs which accompany a worldly domination." This seemed to be characteristic of the spirit with which Mr. Eliot discharged his duties as the pastor of a Church.

An observation of Rev. Samuel Ward has been quoted as applicable to him: "In observing I have observed and found that divers great clerks have had but little fruit of their ministry, but hardly any truly zealous men of God, though of lesser gifts, but have had much comfort of their labors in their own and bordering parishes, being in this likened by Gregory to the iron on the smith's anvil, sparkling round about."

Mather says, "The Lord Jesus Christ was the load-stone which gave a touch to all the sermons of our Eliot; a glorious, precious, lovely Christ, was the point of heaven to which they still verged unto." It is said, that though he printed many books or pamphlets, his heart seemed to be in none of them so much, as in his 'Harmony of the Gospels, in the holy History of Jesus Christ.' It was a standing piece of advice with him to young ministers, "Pray let there be much of Christ in your ministry." On hearing a sermon in which the Saviour had been made prominent, he would say, O, blessed be God, that we hear Christ so much and so well preached in poor New England.

On coming out of the meeting-house where he had been listening to a sermon, he said to the preacher, "Brother, there was oil required for the service of the sanctuary; but it must be beaten oil; I praise God that I saw your oil so well beaten to-day; the Lord help us always by good study to beat our oil that there may be *no knots in our sermons left undissolved*, and that there may a clear light be thereby given in the house of God." Still it is observed that he looked for something more than mere study in a sermon; he required those things in it which would make the hearer feel that the Spirit of God was in the sermon and with the preacher, and he was once heard to complain, "It is a sad thing when a sermon shall have that one thing, The Spirit of God, wanting in it."

He had eminently spiritual views of the duty and privilege of infant baptism. On giving the Rev. Cotton Mather the Right Hand of Fellowship at his ordination, he said to him, "Brother, art thou a lover of the Lord Jesus Christ?

Then I pray, feed his lambs." He was careful to have the lambs pass under the "Lord's tything rod." One Mr. Norcott, a truly pious man, published a book against the baptism of infants, which being circulated in Boston and the vicinity, Mr. Eliot answered it in a brief publication, beginning with these words: "The book speaks with the voice of a lamb, and I think the author is a godly though erring brother; but he acts the cause of a roaring lion, who by all crafty ways, seeketh to devour the poor lambs of the flock of Christ." He then speaks "in the behalf of those who cannot speak for themselves."

On one occasion, speaking of the Saviour's directions to Peter, John 21: 15, he observed, That *the care of the lambs is one third part of the charge over the house of God.*

The title of one of Mr. Eliot's publications, "The Divine Management of Gospel Churches, by the Ordinance of Councils, constituted in order according to the Scriptures, which may be a means of uniting those two holy and eminent parties, the Presbyterians and the Congregational," shows that a plan of union between these two sister denominations is not wholly of modern origin.

But reserving many things respecting Mr. Eliot's character and opinions for another place in this book, let us now look at him in that remarkable work to which God appointed him among the Indians of this vicinity.

CHAPTER IV.

Nonantum. Mather's description of the natives. The Lost Tribes of Israel. Specimen of Indian words. Eliot's first religious exercise at Nonantum. Indian Questions. Second visit to the Indians. Indian Questions. Eliot's reflections on his interviews. Anecdotes.

THE old turnpike road to Worcester, in Brighton, leaves Nonantum hill on the left, and a private road conducts to the summit of the hill which is crowned by two mansions.* The scenery from that hill has a rare combination of still life and of the busy world. The Charles River, seen from a distant part of the hill, meanders to the sea; the quiet, classic scenes of Cambridge are before the eye; soft undulations of hill and dale, winding roads and aboriginal woods, and the quiet waters of the estuary, impress the mind with sensations of repose which are pleasantly broken by the distant noise of travel upon the bridges, the sudden whistle of the locomotive, and an impressive view of the neighboring city. That hill, extending as far as Watertown, and Newton, was once the favorite residence of

* Now owned and occupied by Warren Dutton and Horace Gray, Esqrs.

the Indians, in this vicinity,* and thither Eliot, the pastor of the neighboring Church in Roxbury, directed his way, to give the Indians the word and ordinances of the Gospel in their own language.

Cotton Mather says, "The natives of the country now possessed by the New Englanders, had been forlorn and wretched heathen ever since their first herding here; and though we know not how these Indians first became inhabitants of this mighty continent, yet we may guess that probably the devil decoyed these miserable savages hither, in hopes that the gospel of our Lord and Saviour Jesus Christ would never come here to destroy or disturb his absolute empire over them. But our Eliot was in such ill-terms with the devil, as to alarm him by sounding the silver trumpets of heaven in his territories, and make some noble and zealous attempt towards ousting him of his ancient possessions here. There were, I think, twenty

* "The first place he began to preach at was Nonantum, near Watertown, upon the south side of Charles River, about four or five miles from his own house; where lived at that time, Wabon, one of their principal men, and some Indians with him." Gookin, Mass. Hist. Soc. Coll. for 1792, Vol. I.

"The place where Eliot first began to preach to the Indians, was at Nonantum, a hill at the northeast corner of Newton, nearly where Messrs. Haven's and Wiggin's houses now stand." Moore's Lif of Eliot.

several nations, if I may call them so, of Indians, upon that spot of ground which fell under the influence of our Three United Colonies; and our Eliot was willing to rescue as many of them as he could from that old usurping landlord of America, who is, by the wrath of God, the prince of this world."*

Some of the interest and zeal which many of the first planters and their successors felt with regard to the Indians, was owing to their belief that they were the Ten Tribes of Israel. Cotton Mather enumerates "some small reasons," as he calls them, which led the English to suspect that they might be Israelites. He adds, "They have, too, a great unkindness for our swine;"—but he does not seem to place much reliance on that coincidence with the Jewish antipathy to swine, for he adds, "but I suppose that is because our swine devour their clams, which are a great dainty with them."

This supposition that the North American Indians are the Ten Tribes of Israel, has seemed even more probable to many modern writers than it did to the first settlers of the country. Mr. Catlin, in his interesting and valuable work on the North American Indians, mentions many curious facts in the history, manners and cus-

* Mag. Book III., Part IV. See Appendix, C.

toms of the present race of red men, in favor of this supposition. But there are so many theories on the subject of the Lost Tribes of Israel, and it is so easy for an ingenious mind to discover or invent resemblances, that neither this theory nor any other on the same subject has ever obtained general belief.

It was to a people of rude speech and fierce countenance that Mr. Eliot endeavored to give a knowledge of the Gospel and the institutions of civilized life. His first labor of course was to acquire their language. It was the language of the Massachusetts Indians to which he applied himself. He found an old Indian who could speak English, took him into his family, and by finding out one word, and expression, and sentence after another, he soon was able to converse in that tongue, and finally understood it so well that he reduced it to rules, and made an Indian grammar. One glance at this language will show that it must have been no easy task for a stranger to learn it well enough to converse in it. Some of the words are of enormous length, one of them sometimes filling a whole line. The word for "our loves," is *noowoomantammoorkanunornash.* "Our question" is *Kummogkodonnattootummooetiteaongannunnarash.* "One would think," says Mather, "that these words had been growing ever since Babel unto the dimensions to which they are now extended." Another remark of his on this subject, though it may seem to us to be somewhat in a trifling mood, was undoubtedly written with sober feelings, considering the prevalent superstitions of those times—superstitions with regard to which we greatly err if we suppose them to have been, in those times, peculiar to America.* "I know not," this writer adds, "what thoughts it will produce in my reader, when I inform him that once finding that the demons in a possessed young woman understood the Latin and Greek and Hebrew languages, my curiosity led me to make trial of this Indian language, and the demons did seem as if they did not understand it."

The reason of the great length of these Indian words is understood to be, that instead of having separate words for pronouns and adjectives, the noun or verb expresses them by adding syllables to itself. Mather, who was ready at anagrams and puns, says that the name *Eliot* read backwards, is *t o i l E*, and he thinks that the name corresponds well with the toil of reducing such a language to a grammar. At the close of his Grammar Eliot wrote these words: "Prayers

* He who thinks that a belief in witchcraft, &c., was a peculiarity of New England, should look into Strype's Ecclesiastical Memorials.

and pains through faith in Christ Jesus, will do any thing."

We have from Eliot's own pen a narrative, called "A true relation of our beginnings with the Indians." It was published in London, in 1647, under this title, "The Day breaking, if not the Sun-rising, of the Gospel, with the Indians in New England."

In October, 1646, Eliot, with a few others, having sought the blessing of God, went to Nonantum, for the purpose, as he says, of making known to the Indians the things of their peace. As they approached the wigwams, five or six of the Chiefs met them with English salutations and bid them welcome. The principal wigwam had been previously prepared for the meeting, and many of the Indians were assembled. Eliot and his companions then began with prayer in the English language, not being sufficiently acquainted with the Indian tongue to make suitable religious impressions at first with it upon the minds of the Indians, and besides they wished to let the Indians see that they felt the duty in hand to be serious and sacred, and they had a desire, moreover, as missionaries to offer up a united supplication to God, "with the same request and heart sorrowes," in that place where God was never wont to be called upon.

It was an affecting sight, as we may suppose, to Eliot and his friends, when they ceased from prayer and looked upon the company of Indians sitting in silence, with a mixture of curiosity and seriousness and wildness in their faces. To such an audience Eliot preached in the Indian tongue from Ezekiel 37 : 9. "Prophesy, son of man, and say to the wind, Thus saith the Lord, Come from the four winds, O breath, and breathe upon these slain that they may live."

It is a curious fact that the name of the man* in whose wigwam they were assembled was Waban, and Waban is the Indian name for the wind, so that it seemed to Waban that the message was sent to him, and it proved a means in his conversion. The text from which Mr. Eliot preached on this occasion, was not one which his hearers could at first understand, and therefore some have expressed surprise at the selection of it. But in reply to this, it may be asked, what passage of the Word of God would have been immediately intelligible to those ignorant hearers? Besides, the text seems to have been chosen by Mr. Eliot for a purpose which is certainly proper on special occasions, viz., as a warrant and encouragement to his own soul and

* He was not a Sachem, as frequently stated. See Mass. Hist., Col. IV., 19.

that of his helpers, in preaching in that valley of dry bones. Yet, after suitable religious impressions had been made, and the hearers had felt their lost and wretched state, and their need of divine power, in reflecting upon the text it must have seemed to the hearers peculiarly appropriate to the occasion and to their condition.

An hour and a quarter was occupied in the discourse. Mr. Eliot gave the Indians first a brief exposition of the ten commandments, showing the wrath and curse of God against those who break the least one of them. The subject was then applied, and the law having been brought to do its work in their hearts, and their sins being pointed out to them, as Mr. Eliot says, with much sweet affection, Jesus Christ was preached to them as the only Saviour. He told them who Christ was, and what he did, and whither he had gone, and how he will come again to judge the wicked and burn the world. The creation and fall of man, the greatness of God, heaven and hell, the pleasures of religion and the miseries of sin were then explained in language and with illustrations suited to their capacity.

The sermon being finished, Mr. Eliot proposed some questions to them, and first inquired whether they understood what had been said, and whether all or only some of them understood it? A multitude of voices exclaimed that they all understood every thing which had been spoken. Leave was then granted them to put questions, and it is interesting to notice the first questions which these children of the wilderness proposed. The first questions were,

"What is the cause of thunder?"

"What makes the sea ebb and flow?"

"What makes the wind blow?"

But there were some questions proposed by them which Mr. Eliot says some special wisdom of God directed them to ask, as, for example,

How may we come to know Jesus Christ?

Mr. Eliot told them that if they could read the Bible they would see clearly who Jesus Christ is, but inasmuch as they could not then read, he desired them to remember what he had told them out of the Bible, and to think much and often upon it, when they lay down on their mats in their wigwams and when they rose up, and to go alone in the fields, and woods, and muse on it, and so God would teach them.

He told them that if they would have help from God in this thing, they must begin to pray, and though they could not make long prayers as the English did, yet if they did but sigh and groan, saying, "Lord, make me to know Jesus

Christ for I know him not," and if with all their hearts they persisted in such prayers, they might hope that God would help them. But they were especially to remember that they must confess their sins and ignorance to God and mourn over them and acknowledge how just it would be in God to withhold from them any knowledge of Christ, on account of their sins.

This instruction was communicated to them by Mr. Eliot through the Indian interpreter whom he had brought with him, but he says he was struck with the fact that a few words from the Preacher had much greater effect than many from the interpreter.

One of them asked, whether Englishmen were ever at any time so ignorant of God and Jesus Christ as they themselves?

Another put this question: Whether if the father be naught and the child good, will God be offended with that child? because in the second commandment it is said that he visits the sins of the fathers upon the children.

They were told in reply to this that every child who is good will not be punished for the sins of his father, but if the child be bad, God would then visit his father's sins upon him, and they were bid to notice that part of the second commandment which contains a promise to the thousands of them that love God and keep his commandments.

One of them asked, How is all the world now become so full of people, if they were all once drowned in the flood? This led to the story of the ark and the preservation of Noah.

Mr. Eliot then proposed some questions to them, for example, Whether they did not desire to *see* God, and were not tempted to think there is no God because they could not see him?

Some of them answered, They did desire to see Him if it could be, but they had heard from Mr. Eliot that he could not be seen, and they did believe that though their eyes could not see him, he was to be seen with their soul within.

Mr. Eliot endeavored to confirm them in this impression, and asked them if they saw a great wigwam or a great house, would they think that racoons or foxes built it? or would they think that it made itself? or that no wise builder made it, because they could not see him who made it?

Knowing that the doctrine of one God was a great stumbling block to them, Mr. Eliot asked them if they did not think it strange that there should be but one God, and yet this God be in Massachusetts, and in Connecticut, in Old England, in this wigwam, and the next, and every where at the same time?

One of the most sober of them replied that it was indeed strange, as every thing else they had heard preached was strange, and they were wonderful things which they never heard of before, but yet they thought "it might be true, and that God was so big every where." Mr. Eliot illustrated the truth by the light of the sun, which, though it was but a creature of God, shed its light into that wigwam, and the next, in Massachusetts and Old England, at once.

He inquired of them if they did not find something troubling them within after the commission of murder, theft, adultery, lying; and what would comfort them, and remove that trouble of conscience when they should die and appear before God?

They replied that they were thus troubled, but they could not tell what they should say about it, or what would remove this trouble of mind, whereupon Mr. Eliot enlarged upon the evil of sin and the condition of the soul which is cast out of the favor of God.

Having spent three hours in this interview, Mr. Eliot asked them if they were not weary, and they said, no. But thinking it best to leave them with an appetite, Mr. Eliot concluded the meeting with prayer, but before he departed the principal Indian expressed a desire for more land to build a Town upon, and Mr. Eliot promised to speak for them to the General Court, "that they might possess all the compass of that hill upon which their wigwams then stood."

In the second visit which Mr. Eliot made to the Indians at Nonantum, he began to catechise the younger children. He framed three questions only, that their memories might not be overloaded. The questions and answers were these:

1. Who made you and all the world. Ans. God.

2. Who do you think should save you and redeem you from sin and hell? Ans. Jesus Christ.

3. How many commandments hath God given you to keep. Ans. Ten.

By the time that the questions reached the smaller children, they had learned the answers perfectly, from hearing the others repeat them, and the parents had become familiar with them, and they were requested to use this *Shorter* Catechism of three questions, in teaching their children, against the next visit.

The substance of Mr. Eliot's address to the Indians on this occasion was this: "We are come to bring you good news from the great God Almighty, Maker of Heaven and earth, and to tell you how evil and wicked men may come to be good, so that while they live they may be happy, and when they die may go to God and live in heaven."

He then endeavored to give them just impressions concerning God, his power, greatness, and goodness, his will, what he required of all men, even of the Indians, in the ten commandments, the dreadful punishment of all who break one of these commandments, the anger of God at sin, and yet his compassion for sinners in sending Christ to die for wicked men. He taught them that if they would repent and believe, God would love the poor miserable Indians, but that the wrath of God would burn against all who neglected so great salvation as was now offered to them by those whose only desire was their salvation.

The power of these words was manifestly felt by one of the Indians, who at the thought of his sins and of the danger to which they exposed him, wept aloud, yet without affectation, but striving to conceal his emotions.

Perhaps in no way can we communicate religious instruction in a more simple and effectual way to the young who may read this book, than to record here the questions and answers which Mr. Eliot has preserved in his several interviews with the Indians. Other writers who lived at that time have also recorded questions and answers which they heard. But it will not be necessary to state the times, or places, or the hand by which they were recorded.

An old man rose up after Mr. Eliot had finished his sermon, and asked whether it was not too late for such an old man as he, who was near death, to repent or seek after God.

This question affected Mr. Eliot and his companions with compassion. They told him what is said in the Bible about those who were hired at the eleventh hour, and drew a parallel to his case by describing a son who had for very many years been disobedient, and afterwards penitent, and the feelings of his father towards him.

Question. How came the English to differ so much from the Indians in the knowledge of God and Jesus Christ, seeing they all had at first one father?

Question. How may we come to serve God?

Question. How comes it to pass that the sea water is salt and the land water fresh?

Answer. This is one of the wonderful works of God. As strawberries are sweet and cranberries sour, by the appointment of God, so was it in this case. To this was added some account of natural causes and effects in connection with this subject, "which they less understood, yet did understand somewhat, as appeared by their usual signs of approving what they understand."

Question. If the water is higher than the earth, how comes it to pass that it doth not overflow all the earth?

The missionary took an apple and illustrated the shape of the earth, the motion on its axis, and round the sun; then showed them how God made a great hollow ditch for the waters, which was so deep as to hold the waters by the attraction of gravitation, so that notwithstanding their convexity, they could not overflow the earth.

During a recess in this interview, the Indians were busily employed in discussing these several subjects among themselves, their minds being evidently excited by them, through the effect of new ideas upon subjects which were new or had always been incomprehensible to them. Being afterwards asked if they wished to propose any further questions, one asked,

If a man has committed some great sins, (stolen goods, &c.,) and the Sachem does not punish him, and he is not punished, but he restores the goods, what then? is not all well now? meaning to ask whether restoration made sufficient amends to the law of God.

He was told that though men be not offended at such sins, yet God is angry. The holiness of God was here illustrated. Such a sinner should seek forgiveness as much as any other sinner through the blood of Christ.

Upon hearing this answer, the Indian who proposed the question drew back and hung down his head, with an appearance of great sorrow and confusion, and finally broke out saying, "Me little know Jesus Christ, or me should seek him better." Mr. Eliot comforted him by telling him that as it is early dawn at first when there is but little light, but the sun rises to perfect day, so it would be with him and his people with regard to a knowledge of the favor of God if they would seek Him.

One of the Indians who had received religious impressions in his acquaintance with the colonists, said he would propose this question. A little while since he said he was praying in his wigwam to God and Jesus Christ, that God would give him a good heart; that in his prayer another Indian interrupted him and told him that he prayed in vain, because that Jesus Christ could not understand what Indians speak in prayer; he had been used to hear Englishmen pray, and so could well enough understand them, but Indian language in prayer he was not acquainted with. His question therefore was, "Whether God and Jesus Christ did understand Indian prayers?"

At the close of one interview, Mr. Eliot prayed for above fifteen minutes in the Indian tongue, that they might feel that Christ understood such prayers. The Indians stood about him in grotesque figures, some of them lifting up their eyes and their hands to accompany the prayer, and one of them holding a rag to his eyes and weeping violently, and after prayer retiring to a corner of the wigwam to weep in secret; which one of Mr. Eliot's companions observed and spoke with him, and found him to be deeply affected with a sense of his guilt.

Mr. Eliot makes several useful observations in view of his first two visits to the Indians.

1. None of them slept in sermon or derided God's messenger.

2. That there is need of learning in ministers who preach to Indians more than to gracious Christians, in order to answer their philosophical questions.

3. That there is no need of miraculous or extraordinary gifts in seeking the conversion of the most depraved of the human family.

4. If Englishmen despise the preaching of faith and repentance and humiliation for sin, the poor heathens will be glad of it, and it shall do good to them.

He adds to this, The Lord grant that the foundation of our English woe be not laid in the ruin and contempt of those fundamental doctrines of faith, repentance, humiliation for sin, but rather relishing the novelties and dreams of such men as are surfeited with the ordinary food of the Gospel of Christ. Indians shall weep to have faith and repentance preached, when Englishmen shall mourn, too late, that are weary of such truths.

5. That the deepest estrangement of man from God is no hindrance to his grace, nor to the Spirit of grace. What nation or people ever so deeply degenerated since Adam's fall, as these Indians, and yet the Spirit of God is working upon them.

"It is very likely if ever the Lord convert any of these natives, they will mourn for sin exceedingly, and consequently love Christ dearly; for if by a little measure of light such heart-breakings have appeared, what may we think will be when more is let in?"

"They are some of them very wicked, some very ingenious. These latter are very apt and quick of understanding, and naturally sad and melancholy, (a good servant to repentance) and therefore there is the greater hope of heart-breakings if ever God brings them effectually home, for which we should affectionately pray."

Mr. Eliot says, " It is wonderful to see what a little leaven and that small mustard-seed of the Gospel will do, and how truth will work when the spirit of Christ hath the setting of it on, even upon hearts and spirits most incapable." The night after the Indians had heard the Gospel preached for the third time, an English youth lodged in Waban's tent. He said that Waban instructed his companions with regard to the things which they had heard that day, and prayed with them, and that he awoke several times that night and began to pray and speak to one and another of the Indians of the things which they had heard. Mr. E. says, This man, being a man of gravity and chief prudence, a counsel among them, although no Sachem, is like to be a means of great good to the rest of his company, unless cowardice or witchery put an end, as usually they have done, to such hopeful beginnings.

Two young Indians being at an Elder's house one Sabbath evening, having been previously affected under Mr. Eliot's preaching, one of them began to confess to the elder how wicked he had been, and declared that God could never look upon him with love. The elder opened to him in a familiar manner the truth of God's love to the guilty, his willingness to pardon the vilest through the redemption made by Christ, and illustrated his instructions by the discourse of Christ to the Samaritan woman at Jacob's well, and how Christ forgave her though she was living in sin at the moment when he began to speak to her. Whereupon the young man began to weep bitterly, and the other youth, his companion, disclosing his own guilt, burst out into loud weeping in which they both continued for half an hour.

An old man told Mr. Eliot at one of the meetings that he was fully purposed to keep the Sabbath, but still he was in fear whether he should go to heaven or hell. This was a case in which reliance on good works gave as usual no peace to the conscience. It led Mr. Eliot to speak fully of the way of justification by Christ without works, "as the remedy against all fears of hell."

Mr. Eliot was interested in the fact that some of the Indians who seemed to receive the Gospel most readily, and feel its power, were able to use "gracious expressions," as he calls them, which he was confident they had not heard from him, nor from his assistants. He gives a specimen of them with the corresponding Indian words:

Amanaomen	Jehovah	tahassen	metagh.
Take away,	Lord,	my stony	heart.

Checheson	Jehovah	kekowhogkow.
Wash,	Lord,	my soul.

"What are these," he says, "but the sprinklings of the spirit and blood of Christ Jesus on their hearts? and 'tis no small matter that such dry, barren, and long accursed ground should yield such kind of increase in so small a time. I would not readily commend a fair day before night, nor promise much of such kind of beginnings, in all persons, nor yet in all of these, for we know how the profession of many is but a mere paint, and their best graces nothing but mere flashes and pangs which are suddenly kindled, and as soon to go out, and are extinct again; yet God doth not usually send his plough and seeds-men to a place but there is at least some little piece of good ground, although three to one be naught; and methinks the Lord Jesus would never have made so fit a key for their locks unless he had intended to open some of their doors, and so to make way for his coming in."

At the fourth meeting with the Indians, the children having been catechised, and the vision of the dry bones, which seems to have impressed Mr. Eliot from the first in speaking to the Indians, being explained, they offered all their children to the English to be educated by them.

At this time one of them being asked, What is sin ? he answered, A naughty heart. He did not seem to feel that sin consists only in outward acts.

One of them complained that some of the Indians reviled him and the more serious Indians, calling them rogues, and otherwise insulting them for cutting off their long locks and arranging their hair in a modest manner, for, Mr. Eliot says, " since the word hath begun to work upon their hearts they have discerned the vanity and pride which they placed in their hair, and have therefore, of their own accord (none speaking to them that we know of) cut it modestly." They said that some Indians who had heard the news of the great attention to religion among them, would come from a distance and stay with them three or four days, and one Sabbath, and then they would go from them, (implying that they did not like the Sabbath), but as for themselves, they said they were fully purposed to keep the Sabbath.

Some of the Indians who heard the Gospel, despised and rejected it. So it has always been and is now, wherever the Gospel is preached. Some have their hearts opened to attend to the things of their peace, and others are hardened. Mr. Eliot's assistant, learning that some Indians had discouraged and threatened others with regard to their attendance on the preaching, spoke to them on one occasion about the temptations of Satan. After sermon they proposed these questions:

1. Some Indians say we must pray to the devil for all good, and some to God; may we pray to the devil or no?

2. What does *humiliation* mean, which we hear used so often by the English?

3. Why do the English call us Indians, for before they came here we had another name?

4. What is a spirit?

5. May we believe in dreams?

6. How did the English come to know God so much, and we so little?

At the close of this interview they said that

their great desire was to have a town and to learn to spin.

They believed in the existence of an evil spirit, whom they called Chepian, and who they thought corresponded to the devil in Scripture. They gave the following account of their way in which conjurers or Powows were made: Whenever an Indian had a strange dream in which Chepian appeared to him as a serpent, he would make it known to the rest, and for two days the Indians would dance and rejoice for what the serpent had told him, and he then became a Powow, or one whom the devil favored with his communications. The reader will notice the identity of the form in which they made the devil to appear to them, with the form in which he appeared to our first parents.

CHAPTER V.

Nonantum granted to the Indians by the General Court. First Indian Laws. Eliot's and Shepard's account of the progress of the Gospel among the Indians. Concord Indians. Their laws. Nonantum. Questions and anecdotes. Cape Cod Indians. The Synod at Cambridge, 1648, examine the Christian Indians. "Who made Sack?" Anecdotes and Questions. Order of the General Court, 1647. Regard for the Sabbath. Power of conscience. Questions. Burial of a child. Settlement of Natick. Questions.

THE Indians were desirous of obtaining a grant of land for a permanent settlement, that they might enter upon civilized life. They had bartered their principal places to the English. The General Court purchased of some of the planters, who had bought it of the Indians, the place where their meeting was held, and gave it to them. The Indians inquiring what the name of the place should be they were told it should be Noonatomen (afterwards Nonantum) which signifies *rejoicing*, "because they did rejoice at the word of God, and God did rejoice over them as penitent sinners."

The following is a specimen of their first laws:

1. If any man be idle a week, or at most a fortnight, he shall pay five shillings.

3. If any man shall beat his wife, his hands shall be tied behind him, and he shall be carried to the place of justice to be severely punished.

4. Every young man, if not another's servant, and if unmarried, shall be compelled to set up a wigwam, and plant for himself, and not live shifting up and down to other wigwams.

5. If any woman shall not have her hair tied up, but hang loose or be cut as men's hair, she shall pay five shillings.

7. All those men that wear long locks, shall pay five shillings.

Most of the facts above narrated are contained in a piece written by Mr. Eliot, entitled The Day Breaking if not the Sun Rising of the Gospel with the Indians in New England. It was printed in London, "by Richard Cotes, for Fulk Clifton, and are to be sold at his shop under Saint Margaret's Church, on New-fish Street Hill, 1647."

The same printer in 1648, issued another piece, written by Mr. Thomas Shepard, minister of the Gospel of Jesus Christ, at Cambridge, in New England, called, "The Clear sun-shine of the Gospel breaking forth upon the Indians of New England; or, An Historical Narrative of God's Wonderful Workings upon sundry of the Indians, both Chief Governors and common people, in bringing them to a willing and desired submission to the Ordinances of the Gospel; and framing their hearts to an earnest inquiry after the knowledge of God the father and of Jesus Christ the Saviour of the world." This piece was dedicated by Stephen Marshall, Jeremy Whitaker, Edmund Calamy and nine others, in England, "to the Right Honorable the Lords and Commons assembled in High Court of Parliament, That in you the Representatives of this nation, England might be stirred up to be Rejoycers in and advancers of these promising beginnings." They looked upon the success of the Gospel among the Indians as a fulfillment in part of the promise of God the Father to the Son, "Ask of me, and I will give thee the heathen for thine inheritance, and the uttermost parts of the earth for thy possession." Psalm 2. They remind the Parliament that "God makes man's will of sin serviceable to the advancement of the riches of his own grace. The most horrid act that was ever done by the sonnes of men, the murther of Christ, God made serviceable to the highest purposes of Grace and mercy that ever came upon his breast. Hee suffered Paul to be cast into prison to convert the Jaylor, to be shipwrackt at Milita to preach to the barbarous. So he suffered their (the Pilgrims') way to be stopp'd up here, (in England) and their persons to be banished hence, that hee might open a passage for them in the wilderness, and make them instruments to draw soules to him, who had been so long estranged from Him. The end of the adversary was to suppresse, but God's to propagate, the Gospel, as one saith of Paul, his *blindnesse gave light to whole world.* 'Cœcitas Pauli totius orbis illuminatio.' Acts 9 : 9. It was a long time before God let them (the Pilgrims) see any further end of their coming over than to preserve their consciences, cherish their Graces, provide for their sustenance. But hee let them know it was for some farther arrand that he brought them here, giving them some Bunches of Grapes, some clusters of Figs in earnest of the prosperous successe of their endeavours upon these poor out casts. If the first fruits bee specimens, what will the whole harvest bee? When the East and West shal sing together the song of the Lamb."

Mr. Shepard says that the news of what had been done for the Indians at Nonantum, by the preaching of the Gospel, had reached the Concord Indians, and their Sachem was so much affected by it, that he made application to have the Gospel and its ordinances made known to them. "They craved the assistance of one of the chiefe Indians of Noonanetum (Nonantum,) a very active Indian, to bring in others to the knowledge of God."

Mr. Eliot had already expressed his views * on the subject of a native ministry in these words,—"Nor doe I expect any great good will bee wrought by the English, (leaving secrets to God,—although the English surely begin and lay the first stones of Christ's Kingdom and Temple amongst them) because God is wont ordinarily to convert Nations and peoples by some of their owne country men who are nearest to them, and can best speake, and most of all pity their brethren and countrimen."

A native ministry among the Indians began, in an informal way, much earlier than we have seen it begin among other heathen nations. The North American Indians, though sunk in superstition and wickedness, retained much more of intellectual strength, were more shrewd, and sooner became fit to teach their countrymen than has been the case elsewhere in the

* The Day Breaking &c., p. 15.

history of modern missions. No doubt the climate had much to do with the vigor of mind which the Indians have exhibited. They were far removed from the effeminateness of Eastern nations, and though indolent in their dispositions and habits, their minds when roused by the truth of the Gospel, rose to greater intellectual efforts than have been commonly seen in tribes exposed to the enervating influences of warmer latitudes.

Some quotations from the introduction by Calamy and others, to Mr. Shepard's piece above referred to, will show the spirit of those good men, as well as confirm the fact that the Gospel had done wonders in a short time among the Indians. It was published in 1648, two years after Mr. Eliot had begun his labors with them.

They tell the readers of the effects which the Gospel had wrought among the Indians. "They set up prayers in their families morning and evening, and are in earnest in them. And with more affection they crave God's blessing upon a little parched corn, and Indian stalks than many of us do upon our greatest plenty, and abundance. God is making good that promise, Zeph. 2: 11. I will famish all the gods of the earth, (which he doth by withdrawing the worshipers, and throwing contempt upon the worship,) and men shall worship me alone, every one from his place, even all the isles of the heathens."

They call upon the people of England to read and ponder this remarkable narrative of the work of grace among the North American Savages. "Let these poor Indians stand up incentives to us, as the Apostle set up the Gentiles a provocation to the Jews; who knows but God gave life to New England to quicken Old, and hath warmed them that they might heat us; raised them from the dead, that they might recover us from that consumption, and those sad decays which are come upon us."

"This small Treatise is an Essay to that end, an Indian Sermon; though you will not hear us, possibly when some rise from the dead you will hear them. The main Doctrine it preacheth unto all is to value the Gospel, prize the ministry, loath not your manna, surfeit not of your plenty, be thankful for mercies, fruitful under means: Awake from your slumber, repair your decays, redeem your time, improve the seasons of your peace, answer to cals, open to knocks, attend to whispers, obey commands; you have a name you live, take heed you be not dead, you are Christians in shew, be so in deed: least as you have lost the power of religion, God take away from you the form also."

"And you that are ministers learn by this not to despond, though you see not present fruit of your labors; though you fish all night and catch nothing. God hath a fulness of time to perform all his purposes. And the deepest degeneracies and the widest estrangements from God shall be no bar or obstacle to the power and freeness of his own grace when that time is come."

"And you that are merchants, take incouragement from hence to scatter beams of light, to spread and propagate the Gospel into those dark corners of the earth; whither you traffick you take much from them; if you can carry this to them, you will make them an abundant recompense. And you that are Christians indeed, rejoice to see the Curtains of the Tabernacle inlarged, the bounds of the Sanctuary extended, Christ advanced, the Gospel propagated, and souls saved. And if ever the love of God did centre in your hearts, if ever the sense of his goodness hath begot bowels of compassion in you, draw them forth towards them whom God hath singled out to be the objects of his grace and mercy; lay out your prayers, lend your assistance to carry on this day of the Lord begun among them. The Parents also and many others being convinced of the evil of an idle life, desire to be employed in honest labor, but they want instruments and tools to set them on work, and cast garments to throw upon those bodies that their loins may bless you whose souls Christ hath cloathed. Some worthy persons have given much; and if God shall move the heart of others to offer willingly towards the building of Christ a Spiritual temple, it will certainly remain upon their account when the smallest rewards from God shall be better than the greatest layings out for God."

It will be perceived that this is an appeal in behalf of foreign missions. We will consider some of the facts which Mr. Shepard relates, and to which this appeal is an introduction.

"The awakening of the Indians in our Towne," says Mr. Shepard, "raised a great noyse among all the rest round about us, especially about Concord side, where the Sachim and one or two more of his men hearing of these things, and of the preaching of the Word, and how it wrought among them here, came therefore hither to Noonanetum, (Nonantum,) to the Indian Lecture, and what the Lord spake to his heart wee know not, only it seems he was so farre affected as that he desired to become more like to the English, and to cast off those Indian wild and sinfull courses they formerly lived in; but when divers of his men perceived their Sachim's mind, they secretely opposed him herein, which opposition being known, he therefore called together his chief men about him, and made a speech to this effect unto them, viz.: That they had no reason at all to oppose those courses the English were now taking for their good, for saith hee, all the time you have lived after the Indian fashion, under the power and protection of higher Indian Sachims, what did they care for you? They onely sought their owne ends out of you, and therefore would exact upon you and take away your skins, and your kettles, and your wampam from you at their own pleasure, and this was all that they regarded: but you may evidently see that the English mind no such things, care for none of your goods, but onely seek your good and welfare, and instead of taking away all, are ready to give to you."

The effect of this speech seems to have been happy. The Indians sought the assistance of a discreet and active Indian at Nonantum, "in making certain lawes for their more religious and civill government, and behaviour." It will interest the reader to observe the fruit of this half civilized legislator's advice and labors. Mr. Shepard gives us the "Conclusions and Orders made and agreed upon by divers Sachims and other principall men amongst the Indians at Concord, in the end of the eleventh moneth, An. 1646."* The following are a good specimen of the whole:

1. Every one that shall abuse themselves with rum or strong liquors, shall pay for every time so abusing themselves twenty shillings.

2. There shall be no more Powwowing amongst the Indians. And if any shall hereafter Powwow, both he that shall Powwow, and he that shall cause him to Powwow shall pay twenty shillings apiece.

3. They do desire that they may be stirred up to seek after God.

4. They desire they may understand the wiles of Satan, and grow out of love with his suggestions and temptations.

5. That they may fall upon some better course to improve their time than formerly.

6. That they may be brought to the sight of the sin of lying, and whosoever shall be found guilty herein, shall pay for the first offence five shillings, the second ten shillings, the third twenty shillings.

---

* Shepard's Clear Sunshine, p. 39. Hist. Coll. Vol. IV. 3d series. Shattuck's Hist. Concord.

7. Whosoever shall steale any thing from another, shall restore fourfold.

8. They desire that no Indian hereafter shall have any more but one wife.

9. They desire to prevent the falling out of Indians, one with another, and that they may live quietly one by another.

10. That they may follow after humility, and not be proud.

11. That when Indians doe wrong, they may be liable to censure by fine or the like, as the English are.

12. That they pay their debts to the English.

13. That they doe observe the Lord's day, and whosoever shall prophane it, shall pay twenty shillings.

14. This order refers to the disgusting practice of eating vermin gathered from their persons; "and whosoever shall offend in this case shall pay for every louse a penny."

15. They will weare their haire comely as the English do, penalty five shillings.

16. They intend to reforme themselves in their former greasing themselves, penalty five shillings.

17. They do all resolve to set up prayer in

their wigwams, and to seek God both before and after meate.

20. Whosoever shall play at their former games shall pay ten shillings.

22. Wilful murder shall be punished by death.

23. They shall not disguise themselves in their mournings, as formerly; nor shall they keep a great noyse by howling.

25. No Indian shall take an Englishman's canooe without leave, penalty five shillings.

26. No Indian shall come into any Englishman's house, except he first knock; and this they expect from the English.

27. Whosoever beats his wife, shall pay twenty shillings.

28. If any Indian shall fall out with and beate another Indian, he shall pay twenty shillings.

29. They desire they may be a towne, and either to dwell on this side the Beare swamp, or at the East side of Mr. Flint's Pond.

These orders were put into form by Captain Simon Willard, of Concord, whom the Indians chose to be their Recorder. They were very solicitous that what they agreed upon might be faithfully preserved without alteration. The narrative of these conclusions and orders is signed by Thomas Flint, and Simon Willard.*

Mr. Shepard says that on the 3d March, 1647, he and the Rev. Messrs. Wilson of Boston, Allen, of Dedham, and President Dunster, and many Christian friends, attended the Indian Lecture at Nonantum. "On which day," he says, "perceiving divers of the Indian women well affected, and considering that their soules might stand in need of answer to their scruples as well as the mens, and yet because we knew how unfit it was for women so much as to ask questions publicly immediately by themselves, wee did therefore desire them to propound any questions they would be resolved about by first acquainting either their Husbands or the Interpreter privately therewith; whereupon we heard two questions orderly propounded; which because they are the first ever propounded by Indian women in such an ordinance that ever wee heard of, and because they may bee otherwise useful, I shall therefore set them down."

The first question was proposed by the wife of one Wampooas, a serious Indian, and was to this effect:

"Do I pray when my husband prays, if I

* Shepard's Clear Sunshine, &c., p. 41.

speak nothing as he doth, yet if I like what he says, and my heart goes with it?"

The second was by the wife of one Tothers-wampe, viz., "Whether a husband should do well to pray with his wife, and yet continue in his passions and be angry with his wife?"

Mr. Shepard says, he had "heard few Christians when they begin to look towards God, make more searching questions than these Indians."

An old Indian had an unruly, disobedient son. He asked, "What should one do with him, in case of obstinacy and disobedience, and that will not hear God's word, though his father command him, nor will not forsake his drunkenness, though his father forbid him."

Rev. Mr. Wilson was much moved at this question, "and spake so terribly yet so graciously as might have affected a heart not quite shut up, which this young desperado hearing, (who well understood the English tongue,) instead of humbling himself before the Lord's Word, which touched his conscience and condition so neare, hee was filled with the Spirit of Satan, and as soone as ever Mr. Wilson's speech was ended, he brake out into a loud contemptuous expression. "So!" saith he; which we passed by without speaking againe, leaving the Word with him, which wee knew would one day take its effect one way or other upon him."

In 1647, Messrs. Eliot, Wilson and Shepard, were sent for to Yarmouth, to arbitrate in some difficulties, by means of which "not only that bruised Church, but the whole Towne" was restored to peace. "But Mr. Eliot, as hee takes all other advantages of time, so hee took this, of speaking with, and preaching to the poore Indians in these remote places about Cape Cod."

The Indian dialect varied in forty or sixty miles, and on this account, and because the Indians at Cape Cod "were not accustomed to sacred language, about the holy things of God, wherein Mr. Eliot excels any other of the English, who in the Indian language about common matters excell him," it was difficult to make them understand, yet by the help of one or two interpreters, they succeeded.

There was a Sachem among them of a very furious spirit, whom the English for that reason called Jehu. He promised to attend the preaching on the day appointed, and to bring his men with him, but that very morning he sent his men to sea for fish, and although he came late to hear the Sermon, his men were absent. Yet he feigned that he did not understand what was said, though the others said that he did understand, and Mr. Eliot by privately questioning him found out that he did. He heard, however, "with a dogged look, and a discontented countenance." How curious the uniform resemblance of the human heart in different classes of hearers in every age and place, under the preaching of the Gospel. Who in preaching has not seen a face answering to this Jehu's face, and the heart of man to that of this man?

It was found on this visit to the Indians of Cape Cod, that there was some tradition among them of the Gospel having been preached in those parts before. An aged Indian told the ministers that the very things which Mr. Eliot had taught them as the Commandments of God, and concerning God, and the making of the world by one God, they had heard from some old men now dead. A French ship was wrecked upon that coast many years before, and among the passengers and crew was the Frenchman who, the Indian tradition said,* while the Indians were putting him to death, told them that God was angry with them for their sins. Mr. Shepard speaks of "the French preacher cast upon those coasts many years since." This man may have been a French Catholic Priest,

* See page 19.

on his way to the French possessions in Canada.*

The presence of this preacher among them will account for a dream which one of the Indians related to Mr. Shepard and his companions, as having occurred to him some time ago. The tradition of what the preacher had said, and the account of his appearance was strongly impressed upon his imagination,† as we may suppose, without resorting to any other explanation of the dream which nevertheless is curious and interesting.

He said that two years before the arrival of the English, there was a great mortality in that region, and one night when he was much disturbed and broken of his rest, he dreamed that he saw many men arrive upon the coast, dressed in such clothes as the English wear. Among them there was a man wholly in black, with a thing in his hand which he now saw was an Englishman's book; that the man in black stood on a place higher than the rest, with the English around him, before a great number of the Indians. This man told the Indians that God was *moosquantum*, or angry with them, and would

* See Bancroft's History of the United States, Vol. I.

† See Sir Walter Scott's "Demonology and Witchcraft," Letter II.

kill them for their sins. He said, that he himself then stood up, and asked the man in black what God would do with him and his Squaw and Papooses. The man would not answer him the first nor the second time, but the third time he proposed the question, the man smiled upon him, and told him that he and his papooses would be safe, and that God would give them victuals and other good things.

Strange as it may seem, this dreamer who seemed thus to have had his dream fulfilled, would not come to the sermon till it was nearly finished, and then finding that the man in black was yet speaking, "away he flung," and was seen no more by the ministers till the next day. Whether Satan, or fear, or guilt, or the world prevailed, Mr. Shepard says he could not say.

The next year this writer says, he was much surprised in attending an Indian Lecture at Nonantum, to see so many Indian men, women, and children, in English apparel, so that they were scarcely known from the English people. Partly by gifts, and partly by their own labors, some of them had obtained means by which they were even handsomely dressed.

June 9, 1648, was the first day of the Synod's meeting at Cambridge. The forenoon was spent in hearing a sermon preparatory to the work of the Synod, and the afternoon was occupied in hearing an Indian Lecture. "There was a great gathering of Indians from all parts to hear Mr. Eliot, which we conceived not unseasonable at such a time; partly that the reports of God's worke begun among them might be seen and believed of the chief who were then sent, and met from all the churches of Christ in this country, who could hardly believe the reports they had heard concerning these new stirs among the Indians, and partly hereby to raise up a greater spirit of prayer, for the carrying on the work begun upon the Indians among all the churches and servants of the Lord Jesus. The sermon was spent in showing them their miserable condition without Christ, out of Ephes. 2 : 1, that they were dead in trespasses and sinnes, and in pointing unto them the Lord Jesus who onely could quicken them."

After sermon, opportunity was given for the Indians to ask questions. Some of them were these:

What countryman was Christ, and where was he born?

How far off is that place from us here?

Where is Christ now?

How may we lay hold on Christ, and where, he being now absent from us?

Mr. Shepard continues, " But that which I note is this, that their gracious attention to the Word, the affections and mournings of some of them under it, their sober propounding of divers and spirituall questions, their aptnesse to beleeve and understand what was replyed to them; the readiness of divers poore naked children to answer openly the chief questions in the Catechism, which were formerly taught them, and such like appearances of a great change upon them did marvellously affect all the wise and godly ministers, magistrates and people, and did raise their hearts up to great thankfulnesse to God; very many deeply and abundantly mourning for joy to see such a blessed day, and the Lord Jesus so much known and spoken of among such as never heard of him before: So that if any in England doubt of the truth of what was formerly writ; or if any malignant eye shall question and vilifie this work, they will now speak too late, for what was here done at *Cambridge*, was not set under a Bushell, but in the open Sunne; and what *Thomas* would not beleeve by the reports of others, he might be forced to beleeve by seeing with his own eyes, and feeling Christ Jesus thus risen among them with his own hands."*

An old Indian came to Mr. Eliot's house, as Mr. Eliot told Mr. Shepard, and Mr. Eliot told him that because he brought his wife and children to meeting so constantly, he would give him some clothes, for it was cold weather, and the old man was quite destitute. He did not understand this term which Mr. Eliot used for clothes, and enquired of Mr. Eliot's Indian domestic, and when he understood that it was clothing which was promised, he broke out with much feeling, saying, "God is merciful:"—"a blessed, because a plainhearted, affectionate speech," says Mr. Shepard, "and worthy of Englishmen's thoughts when they put on their clothes; to think that a poor blind Indian that scarce ever heard of God before, that hee should see not only God in his clothes, but mercy also in a promise of a cast off worne sute of clothes, which were then given him, and which he now daily wears."

Mr. S. says that "Mr. Edward Jackson one of our Towne, constantly attended Mr. Eliot's Lectures, and took down the questions and answers, and having sent me his notes, I shall send you a taste of some of them," viz.:

* "Cleare Sunshine of the Gospel," p. 46.

1. Why are some so bad that they hate those men that would teach them good things?

2. Was the devil or man made first?

3. If a father prays to God to teach his sons to know him, and he doth teach them himself, and they will not learn to know God, what should such fathers do? This question was pu by an old man that had rude children.

4. A Squaw asked this question: Whether she might not go and pray in some private place in the woods, when her husband was not at home, because she was ashamed to pray in the wigwam before company?

5. How may one know wicked men, who are good, and who are bad?

6. To what nation did Jesus Christ come first unto, and when?

The following question illustrates the old saying, that a child or fool may ask a question which a philosopher cannot answer. It relates to the solemn and fearful subject of the dissolution of the body and soul. Who has not, at least in his earlier years, puzzled himself with questions about the passage of a departing spirit from the chamber of death? The question referred to was this:

7. If a man should be inclosed in iron a foot thick, and thrown into the fire, what would be-

come of the soul? Could the soul come out thence or not?

8. Why did not God give all men good hearts, that they might be good?

9. If one should be among strange Indians that know not God, and they should make him to fight against some whom he ought not to fight against, and he should refuse, and for his refusal they should kill him, what would become of his soul in such a case? This question was asked by a "stout fellow," whose mind was interested in religion, and was connected with the notion of the Indians that all their valiant men have a reward after death. He seemed to think that his refusal to fight in the case supposed, might prejudice his chance of reward hereafter.

10. How long is it before men believe who have the word of God made known unto them?

11. How may we know when our faith is good, and our prayers good prayers?

12. Why did not God kill the devil, that made all men so bad, God having all power?

13. If we be made weak by sin in our hearts, how can we come before God to sanctify the Sabbath?

An amusing incident took place at one of the public meetings. A drunken Indian cried out,

"Mr. Eliot, who made sack? Who made sack?" This, it will be perceived, was a cavil about the "origin of evil." It is said that "he was soon snib'd by the other Indians, who cried out that it was a papoose question. Mr. Eliot seriously answered him; which hath cooled his boldness ever since."

The man who took down these questions says that "he had some occasion to speak to Waban, (one of the chief men at Nonantum,) about the time of sun-rising, and staying about half an hour, as he came back by one of the wigwams, the man of that wigwam was at prayer, at which he was so much affected that he stopped under a tree to listen; and these passages of Scripture came to his mind while listening to the voice of devotion from the wigwam: 'All the ends of the earth shall remember and turn unto the Lord.' 'O thou that hearest prayer, unto thee shall all flesh come.'"

He says that he had seen an Indian call his children in from the field where they were gathering corn, when he asked a blessing upon the food before them, "with much affection, having but a homely dinner to eat." Mr. Shepard adds, "I wish the like hearts and wayes were seen in many English who professe themselves Christians, and that herein and many the like excellencies they were become Indians, excepting that name, as he did, in another case, except these bonds."

The following is the substance of an order passed by the General Court at Boston, May 26, 1647, concerning the Indians.

" Upon information that the Indians dwelling among us, and submitted to our government, being by the ministry of the Word brought to some civility, are desirous to have a course of ordinary judicature set up among them:

"It is ordered, therefore, by authority of this Court, that some one or more of the magistrates, as they shall agree among themselves, shall, once every quarter, keep a Court at such place where the Indians ordinarily assemble to hear the Word of God, and may then hear and determine all causes civill and criminall, not being capitall, concerning the Indians only; and that the Indian sachims shall have libertie to take order in the nature of summons or atachments, to bring any of their own people to the said Courts, and to keep a Court of themselves every moneth, if they see occasion, to determine small causes of a civill nature, and such smaller criminall causes, as the said magistrates shall refer to them: and the said sachims shall appoint officers to serve warrants, and to execute the orders and judgements of either of said Courts, which officers shall from time to time bee allowed by the said magistrates in the quarter Courts, or by the Governour: And that all fines to bee imposed upon any of the Indians, in any of the said Courts, shall goe and bee bestowed towards the building of some meeting-houses, for education of their poorer children in learning, or other publick use, by the advice of said magistrates, and of Master Eliot, or of such other elder, as shall ordinarily instruct them in the true Religion. And it is the desire of this court that the said magistrates, and Master Eliot, or such other elders as shall attend the keeping of the said Courts, will carefully indeavour to make the Indians understand our most usefull Lawes, and the principles of reason, justice, and equity, whereupon they are grounded; and it is desired that some care may be taken of the Indians on the Lord's dayes."

Mr. Shepard speaks of his brother Eliot as a man "whom, in other respects, but especially for his unweariednesse in this work of God, going up and down among them, and doing them good, I think we can never love nor honor enough." Mr. Eliot says, "That which I first aymed at was to declare and deliver unto them the law of God, to civilize them;

which course the Lord took by Moses, to give the law to that rude company, because of transgression, Galatians 3: 19, to convince, bridle, restrain, and civilize them, and also to humble them. But when I first attempted it they gave no heed unto it, but were weary, and rather despised what I said. A while after God stirred up in some of them a desire to come into the English fashions, and live after their manner, but knew not how to attain unto it; yea, despaired that it should ever come to passe in their dayes; but thought that, in 40 yeears more, some Indians would be all one English, and in an hundred yeears all Indians hereabout would so bee: which when I heard, (for some of them told me they thought so, and that some wise Indians said so,) my heart moved within me, abhorring that wee should sit still and let that work alone, and hoping that this notion in them was of the Lord, and that this mind in them was a preparation to embrace the law and Word of God; and therefore I told them that they and wee were all one save in two things, which make the only difference betwixt them and us: First, wee know, serve, and pray unto God, and they doe not. Secondly, we labor and work in building, planting, clothing ourselves, &c., and they doe not; and would they but doe as wee doe in these things they would bee all one with Englishmen. They said they did not know God, and therefore could not tell how to pray to him nor serve him. I told them if they would learn to know God, I would teach them; unto which they being very willing, I then taught them, (as I sundry times had indeavored afore,) but never found them so forward, attentive, and desirous till this time; and then I told them I would come to their wigwams and teach them, their wives and children, which they seemed very glad of; and, from that day forward, I have not failed to doe that poore little which you know I doe."

Mr. Eliot says that he found the usual opposition to religion among Indians which he found among white men. The Indians of "Dorchester Mill," for example, would not, at first, regard his instructions; "but the better sort of them perceiving how acceptable this was to the English, both to magistrates, and all the good people, it pleased God to step in and bow their hearts, to desire to be taught to know God." "The *Linn* Indians," Mr. Eliot said, "are all naught save one." This was owing to the opposition of their sachem.

A sober Indian going up into the country with two of his sons, prayed as he used to do at home, and talked to the Indians about God and Jesus Christ; whereupon they mocked, and called one of his sons Jehovah, and the other Jesus Christ.

The Nonantum Indians early began to observe the Lord's day. They fined every violator of the Sabbath ten shillings. One Sabbath morning the sachem's wife went to fetch water, when, meeting with other Indian women, she fell into worldly conversation with them, but they reproved her. She insisted that it was not improper, but the other women informed the native Indian preacher who was to address them that day, and he discoursed to them upon the sanctification of the Sabbath, and in his discourse related what he had heard about the sachem's wife. After sermon they had much conversation on the subject, in which the sachem's wife insisted that, inasmuch as her conversation was in private, and early on the Sabbath morning, there was no harm in it; and then she retorted upon the preacher by telling him that he had sinned much more than she in giving occasion to so much talk about this subject on the Sabbath. The whole matter was, by common consent, referred to Mr. Eliot for his arbitration.

Towards evening, on another Sabbath, two

strangers came to Waban's tent (Nonantum); and when they came in, they told him that, about a mile off, they had chased a racoon into a hollow tree, and that if he would send his servants to fell the tree, they might catch him, which Waban, in his desire to entertain the strangers with fresh game, accordingly did. Whereupon the Indians were much displeased, and this case was, by request, made the subject of discourse on the next lecture day.

Another case was this. "Upon a Lord's day their public meeting holding long, and somewhat late when they came at home, in one wigwam the fire was almost out, and therefore the man of the house, as he sat by the fireside, took his hatchet and split a little dry piece of wood, which they reserve on purpose for such use, and so kindled his fire, which, being taken notice of, it was thought to bee such a worke as might not lawfully bee done upon the Sabbath day, and therefore the case was propounded the lecture following for their better information."

A great improvement was soon visible among them in their treatment of their wives. A man who had offended in this respect was brought before the assembly at a time when the governor and many of the colonists happened to be present. The man being publicly accused of beating his wife, made no defence, but confessed his sin, and being kindly admonished and instructed, he turned his face to the wall and wept; "and such was the modest, penitent, and melting behaviour of the man that it much affected all to see it in a barbarian, and all did forgive him; onely this remained, that they executed their law notwithstanding his repentance, and required his fine, to which he willingly submitted, and paid it."

The power of conscience among them is illustrated by Mr. Eliot in the two following anecdotes.

The son of a sachem, 14 or 15 years old, had been intoxicated; and being reproved by his father and mother for disobedient and rebellious conduct, he despised their admonition. Before Mr. E. heard of it, he had observed that on being catechised, the fifth commandment being required of him, he reluctantly said, "Honor thy father," but left out "mother."

George, the Indian, who asked, in a public meeting, "Who made sack?" killed a cow, and sold it at the college for a moose. President Dunster was unwilling that he should be directly charged with it, but wished Mr. Eliot to inquire of him as to the crime. But being brought before the assembly, he freely confessed his sin.

The Indians were never weary of asking

questions in the public meetings. An old Pow-aw once demanded, Why, seeing the English had been in the land twenty-seven years, they had never taught the Indians to know God till now? He added, many of us have grown old in sin, whereas had you begun with us earlier, we might have been good.

The answer was that the English did repent that they were not more earnest at the first to seek their salvation, but the Indians were never willing to hear till now, and as God has now inclined their hearts to hear, the English were striving to redeem the time.

Another question was of deep interest. One of them said, That before he knew God, he thought he was well, but since, he had found his heart to be full of sin, and more sinful than it ever was before; and that this had been a great trouble to him; that at that day his heart was but little better than it was at first, and *he was afraid it would be as bad as it was before, and therefore he sometimes wished that he might die before he should be so bad again!* Now, said he, my question is, Is this wish a sin? Mr. E. says this question was evidently the result of his own experience and seemed to be sincere.

Another question was this:

Whither do our little children go when they die, seeing they have not sinned?

This led to an exposition of the depravity of man's nature, and of the part which it is hoped dying infants have in the redemption made by Christ, and the covenant relation of the children of believers, which last doctrine Mr. Eliot says, "was exceedingly grateful unto them."

The whole assembly at one time united and sent a question to Mr. Eliot by his man, as their united question, viz:

"Whether any of them should go to heaven, seeing they found their hearts full of sin, and especially full of the sin of lust?" At the next lecture held at "Dorchester mill," occasion was taken to preach to them from Matt. 11: 28, 29. "Come unto me all ye that labor and are heavy laden," &c., when the justifying grace of Christ to all who are weary and sick of sin was fully and earnestly set forth. But at this time they repeated their fearful apprehension that "none of them would go to heaven."

A question which uniformly troubled all who began to think of embracing religion was this:

"If we leave off Powawing and pray to God, what shall we do when we are sick?" For though they had some knowledge of the medicinal qualities in certain roots and herbs, they of course had no knowledge of the human system, and hence no skill in applying their remedies, but relied on the antics and unearthly gestures and incantations of their Powaws to make the medicines take effect. Mr. Eliot expressed the desire that the Lord would stir up the hearts of some people in England to give some maintenance towards a school or academy, wherein there should be "Anatomies, and other instructions that way." Mr. E. had himself showed them an anatomy, the only one he says the English had ever had in the country. By a course of instruction in medicine Mr. E. believed that he could most effectually, and perhaps, in the only way, "root out their Powaws."

The Indians proposed this question to Mr. Eliot:

"What shall we say to some Indians who say to us, What do you get by praying to God, and believing in Jesus Christ? You go naked still, and are as poor as we. Our corn is as good as yours; and we take more pleasure than you; if we saw that you got any thing by praying to God, we would do so."

Mr. E. answered to them on this point as follows: "First, God gives two sorts of good things; 1. little things, which he showed by his little finger, ('for they use and delight in demonstrations ;') 2. great things, (holding up his thumb). The little mercies he said are riches, clothes, food, sack, houses, cattle, and pleasures, all which serve the body for a little while, and in this life only. The great mercies are wisdom, the knowledge of God, Christ, eternal life, repentance and faith ; these are for the soul, and eternity. Though God did not give them so many little things, through the knowledge of the Gospel, he gave them the greater things which are better. This he proved by an illustration : when *Foxun*, the Mohegan Counselor, who is counted the wisest Indian in the country, was in the Bay, I did on purpose bring him unto you ; and when he was here, you saw he was a fool in comparison of you, for you could speak of God, and Christ, and heaven, &c. ; but he sat and had not one word to say unless you talked of such poor things as hunting, wars, &c."

He also told them that they had some more clothes than the wicked Indians; and the reason why they had so few, was because they had so little wisdom; but if they were wise to obey God's commands, for example, " Six days shalt thou labor," they would have clothes, houses, cattle, and riches, as the English have.

Many questions and cases of dispute arose

out of their old practice of gaming, to which they were greatly addicted. The irreligious Indians demanded the old stakes of some who had been convinced of the sin of gaming, and had declined to pay their forfeits. The winners however, insisted on being payed. Mr. Eliot had no little trouble in settling the matters of casuistry and conscience which thus occurred. But he took this method in many cases. He prevailed on the creditor to accept one half of his demand, having first showed him the sinfulness of gaming. He then told the debtor in private that God requires us to fulfill our promises though to our hurt, and then asked him if he would pay half. In this way such cases were many of them settled, for the creditors refused Mr. Eliot's proposition, that whoever challenged a debt incurred by gaming should go before the Governor with his demand.

The demand upon Mr. Eliot for agricultural and other implements soon increased beyond his ability to supply them. The women were desirous of learning to spin; wheels were procured for them. The men began to supply the English market all the year round, in the winter with brooms, staves, eel-pots, baskets, and turkies; in the spring with cranberries, fish, and strawberries; in the summer, with whortleberries, grapes and fish; and in the autumn, with cranberries, fish and venison. Some of them worked with the English in haying time, and harvest; but it was hard work for them with their old habits of indolence. "Old boughs," says Mr. Eliot, "must be bent a little at once; if we can set the young twigges in a better bent, it will bee God's mercy."

Mr. Eliot fell in with a Narragansett Sachem, and having spoken to him on the subject of religion, asked him if he did not believe such things? The Sachem seemed averse to answer, and Mr. E. asked him why he had not profited more by the instructions of a Mr. Williams, their teacher? He answered that the Indians did not care to learn of him, because he is no good man, but goes out and works upon the Sabbath day. "I name it," says Thomas Shepard, "not to show what glimmerings nature may have concerning the observation of the Sabbath, but to show what the ill example of the English may do, and *to show what a stumbling-block to all religion the loose observation of the Sabbath is.*"

In a few years Mr. Eliot says a visible improvement had taken place in many of the domestic habits of the Indians, indicating an advancement in the principles and sentiments of civilization. Not only were they as a general thing respectably clothed, but the common wigwams at Nonantum equalled those of Sachems in other tribes, and instead of herding together in one room they made divisions and apartments in their houses from feelings of propriety and modesty.

Questions relating to the plurality of their wives perplexed them, and gave occasion for the same judicious decisions on this delicate and trying subject which are now made by our wise and discreet missionaries in lands where the same practice exists. While some good men are in favor of driving the ploughshare at once among the roots of this and every other evil in the institutions and customs of corrupt society, it is found impracticable to do so, by those who see the complicated nature of these practices, without occasioning still greater evils. Remedial measures are in operation among the converts from heathenism and paganism by which caste and polygamy and other social evils will in time, but not in a day or year, be done away. The process of cure was more rapid among the Indians, than it is among the Oriental tribes, for reasons connected with the character of the people, the ascendency which religion soon had among them, and the absence of opposing influences in the government of the tribes.

The text from which Mr. Eliot preached his first sermon at Nonantum, ("Prophesy to the wind," &c.) and which made Waban, whose name translated, is, the wind, had produced decided effect on him, and he became useful in diffusing the knowledge of the Gospel to other tribes, at Concord, at places on the Merrimack, and elsewhere. He remained steadfast in the faith, and never ceased to think that the Word of God was directed specially to himself in that first sermon of Mr. Eliot, though Mr. E. says that he had no design in the coincidence between the text and the Indian's name.

Mr. Eliot once preached to the Indians from these words, Ephes. 5: 11, "Have no fellowship with the unfruitful works of darkness," &c. One of the questions proposed after sermon was this:

What do Englishmen think of Mr. Eliot, because he comes among wicked Indians to teach them?

Another question was as follows:

Suppose two men sin. The one knows he sinneth, and the other doth not know sin, will God punish both alike?

Another asked, Suppose there should be one

wise Indian that teacheth good things to other Indians, whether should not he be as a father or brother unto such Indians he so teacheth in the ways of God?

One of the Indians at Nonantum had a child sick of consumption. When it was dead some of the Indians came to one of the English and asked him the proper manner of burial. Whereupon the father procured some pieces of board and nails, and made a decent coffin; and about forty of the tribe went with the body to the grave. There having laid the body in the earth, in a solemn and suitable manner, without any howlings, or heathenish rites, or savage gesticulations, they made up the mound, and then of their own accord, for it was not the English custom, they assembled for prayer near the grave, and requested one of their number, a serious Indian by the name of Totherswamp, to pray with them, which he did, "with such zeal and variety of gracious expressions, and abundance of tears, both of himself and most of the company, that the woods rang again with their sighs and prayers."

Thomas Shepard says, "I know that some will think that all this work among them is done and acted thus by the Indians to please the English, and for applause from them; and it is not unlikely but 'tis so in many, who doe but blaze for a time; but certainly 'tis not so in all, but that the power of the Word hath taken place in some, and that inwardly and effectually, but how far savingly time will declare. Some may say that if it be so, yet they are but few that are thus wrought upon. Be it so; yet so it hath ever been, many called, few chosen, and yet withal, I believe the calling in of a few Indians to Christ, is the gathering home of many hundreds more, considering what a vast distance there hath been between them and God so long, even dayes without number; considering also, how precious the first fruits of America will be to Jesus Christ, and what seeds they may be of harvests in after times; and yet if there was no great matter seen in those of grown years, their children, notwithstanding, are of great hopes, both from English and Indians themselves, who are therefore trained up to schoole, where many are very apt to learne, and who are also able readily to answer to the questions propounded, containing the principles and grounds of all Christian religion in their own tongue. I confesse it passeth my skill to tell how the Gospel should be generally received by these American natives, considering the variety of languages in small distances of places; onely hee that made their eares and tongues can raise up some or other to teach them how to heare, and what to spake; and if the Gospel must ride circuit, Christ can and will conquer by weake and dispicable meanes, though the conquest perhaps may be somewhat long."*

Mr. Eliot wrote an interesting letter to a friend in England, dated Roxbury, this 12th of Nov. 1648, and sent it *by the way of Virginia, and through Spain.*

He says that the Indians used to abhor the remembrance of their dead friends, but that now they had begun to receive profit from the recollection of their dying counsels, and hope from their confidence in the safety of the pious dead. The woman who asked the question, whether, when her husband prayed, if she prayed in her heart, but did not speak, yet her heart liked what he said, it was prayer; called her two grown up daughters to her when she was dying and said to them: "I shall now die, and when I am dead, your grand-parents and uncles will send for you to come live among them and promise you great matters, and tell you what pleasant living it is among them. But do not

* Shepard's "Cleare Sunshine."

believe them, and I charge you never hearken unto them, nor live among them; for they pray not to God, keep not the Sabbath, commit all manner of sins, and are not punished for it. But I charge you live here, for here they pray unto God, the Word of God is taught, sins are suppressed and punished by laws, and therefore I charge you live here all your days." Soon after it came to pass as she had said, and the case was propounded to Mr. Eliot, and the father-in-law opposed the removal of the children, on the ground of their mother's charge.

The settlement of Natick took place in the following way. Many Indians in the country were desirous of hearing the Gospel, but they would not remove into the neighborhood of the English, "because they had no tools or skill, or heart to fence their grounds," and so their corn was spoiled by the English cattle, and the English refused to pay for it, because the Indians would not build fences. "Therefore," Mr. E. says, "a place must be found (both for this and sundry other reasons) somewhat remote from the English;—but I feare it will bee too chargeable, though I see that God delighteth in small beginnings that his name may be magnified."

There was a great fishing place at the falls of the Merrimack where the Indians assembled every spring, and Mr. E. visited them. They put a question to him after one of his sermons, which all who are interested in the conversion of the heathen often find occurring to them with painful interest. "If it be thus as you teach, then all the world of Indians are gone to hell, to be tormented forever, until now a few may go to heaven and be saved; is it so?"

In the letter which went so far in getting to England, Mr. Eliot records some further questions from his Nonantum Indians, viz:

How many good people were in Sodom when it was burnt?

Doth the devil dwell in us as we dwell in a house?

When God saith, Honor thy father, doth he mean three fathers, our father, our Sachem, and our God?

When the soul goes to heaven, what doth it say when it comes there. And what doth a wicked soul say when it cometh into hell?

If one sleep on the Sabbath at meeting, and another awaketh him, and he be angry at it, and say it's because he is angry with him that he so doth, is not this a sin?

If any talk of another man's faults and tell others of it when he is not present to answer, is not that a sin?

Why did Christ die in our stead?

Seeing Eve was first in sin, whether she did die first?

Why must we love our enemies, and how shall we do it?

When every day my heart thinks I must die and go to hell for my sins, what shall I do in this case?

May a good man sin sometimes? Or may he be a good man and yet sin sometimes?

If a man think a prayer, doth God know it, and will he bless him?

Who killed Christ?

If a man be almost a good man and dieth, whither goeth his soul?

How long was Adam good before he sinned?

Seeing we see not God with our eyes, if a man dream that he seeth God, doth his soul then see him?

Did Adam see God before he sinned? Shall we see God in heaven?

If a wicked man pray, whether doth he make a good prayer? Or when doth a wicked man pray a good prayer?

Whether God did make hell before Adam sinned?

If two families dwell in one house, and one

prayeth and the other not, what shall they that pray do to them that do not?

Did Abimelech know Sarah was Abraham's wife?

Did not Abraham sin in saying she was my sister?

Seeing God promised Abraham so many children, like the stars for multitude, why did he give him so few? And was it true?

If God made hell in one of the six days, why did God make hell before Adam sinned?

How shall I bring mine heart to love prayer?

If one man repent and pray once in a day, another man often in a day, whether doth one of them go to heaven, the other not? Or what difference is there?

I find I want wisdom, what shall I do to be wise?

Why did Abraham buy a place to bury in?

Why doth God make good men sick?

How shall the Resurrection be, and when?

Do not Englishmen spoil their souls to say a thing cost them more than it did? and is not all one as to steal?

You say our body is made of clay; what is the sun and moon made of?

If one be loved of all Indians, good and bad,

another is hated of all, saving a few that be good, doth God love both these ?

I see why I must fear hell and do so every day. But why must I fear God ?

How is the tongue like fire, and like poison ?

What if false witnesses accuse me of murther, or some foul sin ?

What punishment is due to liars ?

If I reprove a man for sin, and he answer, "Why do you speak thus angrily to me ? Mr. Eliot teacheth us to love one another ?"—is this well ?

Why is God so angry with murtherers ?

If a wife put away her husband because he will pray to God and she will not, what is to be done in this case ?

If there be young women pray to God, may such as pray to God marry one that will not pray to God, or what is to be done in this case ?

Whether doth God make bad men dream good dreams ?

What is salvation ?

What is the Kingdom of Heaven ?

If my wife do some work in the house on the night before the Sabbath, and some work on the Sabbath night, whether this is a sin ?

If I do a sin, and do not know it is a sin, what will God say to that ?

Is faith set in my heart or in my mind?

Why have not beasts a soul as man hath, seeing they have love, anger, &c., as man hath?

How is the Spirit of God in us, and where is it?

Why doth God punish in hell for ever? man doth not so, but after a time lets them out of prison again. And if they repent in hell, why will not God let them out again?

How shall I know when God accepts my prayers?

How doth Christ make peace between man and God? and what is the meaning of that point?

Why did the Jews give the watchmen money to tell a lie?

If I hear God's word when I am young, and do not believe, but when I am old I believe, what will God say?

In wicked dreams doth the soul sin?

Doth the soul in heaven know things done here on earth?

Doth the soul in heaven remember what it did here on earth before he died?

If my heart be full of evil thoughts, and I repent and pray, and a few hours after it is full again, and I repent and pray again; and if after this it be full of evil thoughts again, what will God say?

Why did the earth shake at Christ's resurrection?

What if a minister wear long hair, as some other men do, what will God say?

If a man will make his daughter marry a man whom she doth not love, what will God say?

Why doth Christ compare the kingdom of heaven to a net?

Why doth God so hate them that teach others to commit sin?

CHAPTER VI.

Letters respecting the Indians, from individuals in New England, to their friends in Old England. Speculations about the lost tribes of Israel. Remarks. Questions. Samuel Gorton, the Familist. Two Indians controvert his opinions. Interesting conversation. Labors of the Mayhews on Martha's Vineyard. Covenant of the Indians of Martha's Vineyard. Questions. Merrimack Indians. Accounts by the Mayhews of their labors. Questions.

Some of Mr. Eliot's letters respecting the Indians were published in London, with an appendix by Rev. "J. D." As we are interested and entertained occasionally by a supposed discovery of the lost tribes of Israel, it may not be useless to give here some of the speculations and reasonings of this good man, on this subject as relating to the North American Indians. He begins his appendix with the following words:

"The works of the Lord are great, sought out of all them that love them, saith the Psalmist; Ps. 111: 3. The word which we, render *sought out,* hath a mighty emphasis in it: 'Tis a word used sometimes to denote the elaborate care of digging and searching into mines. And sometimes it's made use of to expresse the

13*

accurate labors of those who comment upon writings. Indeed, there is a golden mine in every work of God; and the foregoing letters to a gracious eye, are as a discovery of a far more precious mine in America, than those gold and silver mines of India: For they bring tidings of the unsearchable riches of Christ, revealed unto poore soules in those parts. . . . . . . I could not pass over so rich a mine without digging.

. . . . "The general consent of many judicious and godly divines doth induce considering minds to believe that the conversion of the Jews is at hand. It's the expectation of some of the wisest Jews now living, that about the year 1650, Either we shall be Mosaick or else that themselves Jews shall be Christians. . . . . There may be at least a remnant of the generation of Jacob in America, (peradventure some of the Ten tribes dispersions.) And that those sometimes poor now precious Indians may be as the first fruits of the glorious harvest of Israel's redemption. The observation is not to be slighted, (though the observer, Mr. Shepard, said it was more cheerful than deep) that the first Text out of which Mr. Eliot preached, was about the dry bones. . . . . . Why may we not at least conjecture, that God by a special finger pointed out that text to be first opened, which immediately concerned the persons to whom it was preached?"

He then states the reasons why the Indian tribes may be of Jewish descent, viz:

"1. They have at least a traditional knowledge of God, as the Maker of heaven and earth.

2. Whatever they attribute unto others, this they peculiarly attribute unto God, viz: that all things, both good and evil, are managed by his Providence.

3. Before they had received any instruction from the English, upon observation of a bad year, or other ill success, they did meet and weep as unto God, and on the other side, upon a good year, or good success in any business, as of War, they used to meet and make a kind of acknowledgement of thanks to God in it.

4. They are careful to preserve the memory of their families, mentioning Uncles, Grand-parents, &c. A thing which had a great tang of, and affinity to, the Jews' care of preserving the memorial of their Tribes.

5. Those of them who have been wrought upon, tell of some face of Religion, wisdom and manners which long agoe their ancestors had, but that it was lost.

6. The better and more sober of them de-

light much to expresse themselves in parables, a thing peculiar to the Jews.

These and the like considerations prevail with me to entertain (at least) a conjecture that these Indians of America may be Jews, especially of the Ten Tribes. And therefore to hope that the work of Christ among them may be as preparatory to his own appearing."

Some of these reasons appertain with equal force to other tribes of the earth who have been supposed by different writers to be remnants of the house of Israel. While we should respect the interest and zeal of those who study the providence of God, with a view to finding out his designs, and to be prepared for the fulfillment of his promises, we should not easily yield our confidence to any hypothesis which rests merely on conjecture, or depends for support in reasons which apply equally well to theories inconsistent with it. This is not the place to remark at large on the interesting subject of the Jews and their conversion, but the impression seems happily to be extending that the sooner we cease to regard them as destined to a national conversion, and look at them as sinners of the human family, like Mohammedans and Papists, and refrain from efforts and a treatment which foster their spirit of separation and their assumption of superior dignity and special claims to respect and favor, the sooner we shall employ ourselves in efforts to address them in a way which will be far more likely to humble their pride, and prepare them to submit to the Gospel, than the somewhat adulatory and flattering method of approaching them and speaking of them will ever be.

The improvement which the writer above named makes of Mr. Eliot's letters in the following exhortations is far more obviously correct than his speculations about the origin and destiny of the Indians. He says the work of grace among them should lead the people of England,

" First, To study and search into the works of the Lord, to see how he counter plots the enemy in his designs; In making the late Bishops persecuting of the godly tend to the promoting of the Gospel.

Secondly, To take heed of despising the day of small things.

Thirdly, To be ashamed of and bewail our want of affection to and estimation of that glorious Gospel, and those great things of Christ, which these poor Heathens upon the little Glymmerings and tasts so exceedingly value and improve.

Fourthly, Doth not the observation of the

preceding reports clearly confirm the doctrine of the Sabbath, and the practice of prayer. O tremble, ye Sabbath slighters and duty despisers, Christ hath witnesses against you in America. . . . . . . The converted Heathen in New England goe beyond you, O ye Apostolic Christians in England.

Arise ye heads of our Tribes in Old England, and extend your help to further Christ's labourers in New England.

Rouse up yourselves, my Brethren! ye preachers of the Gospel, this work concerns you. Contrive and plot, preach for and presse the advancement hereof.

Come forth ye masters of money, part with your gold to promote the Gospel. If you give any thing yearly, remember Christ will be your Pensioner. If you give any thing into banke, Christ will keep account thereof and reward it."

The reader, it is to be hoped, will not be weary of the Indian questions, which Mr. Eliot sent to his friends in England as often as he wrote to them. These questions are not only curious, but they suggest valuable thoughts and lead to profitable reflections.

If a man know God's Word, said one of them at the Indian lecture, but believe it not, and he teach others, is that good teaching? and if others believe that which he teacheth, is that believing or faith? Upon this question Mr. Eliot asked them how they could tell when a man knoweth God's Word, that he doth not believe it? They answered, When he doth not do in his practice answerable to that which he knoweth.

If I teach on the Sabbath that which you have taught us, and forget some, is that a sin? and some I mistake and teach wrong, is that a sin?

Do all evil thoughts come from the devil, and all good ones from God?

What is watchfulness?

What should I pray for at night, and what at morning, and what on the Sabbath day?

What is true Repentance? or how shall I know when this is true?

How must I wait on God?

Shall we see Christ at the day of judgment?

When I pray for a soft heart, why is it still hard?

You said, God promised to go with Moses; how doth he go with us?

When such die as never heard of Christ, whither do they go?

When the wicked die, do they first go to

heaven to the judgment-seat of Christ to be judged, and then go away to hell?

Why doth God say, I am the God of the Hebrews?

When Christ arose, whence came his soul? When it was replied, From heaven; they said, How then was Christ punished in our stead? or when did he suffer in our stead, afore death, or after?

When I pray every day, why is my heart so hard still, even as a stone?

If one purposeth to pray, and yet dieth before that time, whither goeth his soul?

Why must we be like salt?

Doth God know who shall repent, and who not?—why then did God use so much meanes with Pharaoh?

What meaneth that 'blessed are they that mourn'?

When I see a good example, and know that it is right, why do I not do the same?

What anger is good, and what is bad?

Do they dwell in separate houses in heaven, or all together, and what do they?

If a child die before he sin, whither goeth his soul? 'By this question,' says Mr. E., 'it did please the Lord to convince them of original sin, blessed be his name.'

If one that prays to God sins like him that prays not, is not he worse? 'And while,' says Mr. Eliot, 'they discoursed of this point, and about hating wicked persons, one of them shut it up with this: They must love the man and do him good, but hate his sin.'

Why do Englishmen so eagerly kill all snakes?

May a man have good words and deeds, and a bad heart, and another have bad words and deeds, and yet a good heart?

What is it to eate Christ's flesh, and drink his blood; what meaneth it?

What meaneth a new heaven and a new earth?

If but one parent believe, what state are our children in?

How doth much sinne make grace abound?

What meaneth that, We cannot serve two masters?

Can they in Heaven see us here on earth?

Do they see and know each other? Shall I know you in heaven?

If all the world be burnt up, where shall hell be?

Do they know each other in Hell?

What meaneth, that Christ meriteth eternal life for us?

What meaneth that, The woman brought to

Christ a box of oyle, and washt his feet with tears, &c.?

What meaneth that of the two debtors, one oweth much, another but little?

What meaneth God when he sayes, yee shall be my jewels?

If so old a man as I repent, may I be saved?

When we come to believe, how many of our children doth God take with us, whether all, only young ones, or at what age?

What meaneth that, Let the trees of the wood rejoice?

What meaneth that, The Master doth not thank his servant for waiting on him?

When Englishmen choose magistrates and ministers, how do they know who be good men that they dare trust?

Seeing the body sinneth, why should the soul be punished, and what punishment shall the body have?

If a wicked man prayeth and teacheth, doth God accept, or what saith God?

If a man be wise and his Sachem weak, must he yet obey him?

We are commanded to honour the Sachem, but is the Sachem commanded to love us?

When all the world is burnt up, what shall be in the room of it? (By an old woman.)

Mr. Eliot says, in a letter containing these questions, "You may perceive many of the questions arise out of such texts as I handle, and do endeavour to communicate as much Scripture as I can. The word of the Lord converteth, sanctifieth, and maketh wise the simple; sometimes they aske weaker questions than these, which I mention not; you have the best, and when I am about writing, I am careful in keeping a remembrance of them; it may be the same question may be again and again asked at several places and by several persons. The Lord teach them to know Christ, whom to know is eternal life. I shall entreat your supplications at the throne of grace, under the tender wing whereof I now leave you, being forced by the time, and rest,

Your respectful and loving
brother and fellow-laborer
in the Indian work,
JOHN ELIOT."

Samuel Gorton, charged with being a Familist and Antinomian, was banished from Plymouth, Rhode Island, and Massachusetts. The Familists were an Anabaptist sect, founded in Holland, in 1555, by Henry Nicholas, a Westphalian. They held that the essence of religion consists in the feelings of divine love, (and hence they were called the Family of love, and familists), that all other religious tenets, whether relating to matters of faith or modes of worship, are of no consequence, and that it is indifferent what opinions Christians entertain concerning God, provided their hearts are filled with the emotions of piety and love. They were confuted by Dr. Henry More, and by George Fox, the Quaker. A proclamation was issued against them by Queen Elizabeth in 1580.

This Gorton in 1650 was in Rhode Island. Two of the Nonantum Indians made a visit to Providence and Warwick, and spent a Sabbath and heard Gorton and his followers explain their views, and afterwards had some conversation with them.

Upon their return, on a lecture day, before the people had fully assembled, these two Indians addressed a question to Mr. Eliot; and the conversation which ensued is recorded by him as illustrating the proficiency in Christian knowledge to which some of the Indians had attained, and their ability to withstand false teachers.

The question was this: What is the reason that seeing those English people, where they had been, have the same Bible that Mr. Eliot has, yet do not speak the same things? Being asked the reason of his question, they said, They had been at Providence and Warwick, and they perceived by conversation with them that they differed from Mr. E.; they heard their public exercises, but did not understand what they meant, though they understood the English language well. Being asked what they said, they replied, they said thus:

They (that is Mr. Eliot and his friends) teach you that there is a heaven and a hell, but there is no such matter.

Mr. E. asked them what reason they gave for this assertion.

Because there is no other heaven but what is in the hearts of good men, and no other hell but what is in the hearts of bad men.

Mr. E. What did you say to that?

Indians. We told them we did not believe them, because heaven is a place where good men go when this life is ended, and hell is a place where bad men go when they die, and cannot be in the hearts of man.

Mr. E. approving this answer. What else did they say?

Indians. They spake of Baptism, and said, they teach you that infants must be baptized, but that is a very foolish thing.

Mr. E. What reason did they give?

Indians. Because infants neither know God nor baptism, nor what they do, and therefore it is a foolish thing to do it.

Mr. E. What did you say to that?

Indians. I could not say much; but I thought it was better to baptize them while they be young, and then they are bound and engaged; but if you let them alone till they be grown up, it may be they will fly off, and neither care for God nor Baptism.

Mr. E. commended this reply. What further did they say?

Indians. They spake of ministers, and said, they teach you that you must have ministers, but that is a needless thing.

Mr. E. Why?

Indians. They gave these reasons: First, ministers know nothing but what they learn out of God's book, and we have God's book as well as they, and can tell what God saith. Again, ministers cannot change men's hearts, God must do that, therefore there is no need of ministers.

Mr. E. What did you reply?

Indians. I told them that we must do as God commands us, and if he commands us to have ministers we must have them. And further, I told them I thought it was true that ministers cannot change men's hearts; but when we do as God bids us, and hear ministers preach, then God will change our hearts.

Mr. E. What else did they speak of?

Indians. They said, they teach you that you must have magistrates, but that is needless.

Mr. E. What reason did they give?

Indians. They said, Because magistrates cannot give life, therefore they may not take away life; besides, when a man sinneth, he doth not sin against magistrates; and therefore why should they punish them? but they sin against God, and therefore we must leave them to God to punish them.

Mr. E. What answer did you make?

Indians. I said to that as to the former, we must do as God commands us. If God commands us to have magistrates, and commands them to punish sinners, then we must obey.

In answer to the question, Why all who have the Bible do not speak the same things. Mr. E. preached on that occasion from 2 Thes. 2: 10, 11. "Because they believed not the truth that they might be saved; for this cause God shall send them strong delusions that they might believe a lie," &c.

The Rev. Thomas Mayhew, and his son the

Rev. Experience Mayhew, prosecuted the work of evangelizing the Indians of Martha's Vineyard with signal success. As the relations which they give respecting the Indians, and the progress of the Gospel among them, correspond so nearly with the foregoing narratives, it is not thought necessary to speak of them at large. Some idea of the principles which were inculcated by the Mayhews, and of the influence which they exerted upon the natives, may be derived from the following covenant which Mr. Thomas Mayhew wrote for them, and in which they all with free consent willingly and thankfully joined.

COVENANT OF THE INDIANS OF MARTHA'S VINEYARD.

"Wee, the distressed Indians of the Vineyard, (or NOPE, the Indian name of the Island,) that beyond all memory have been without the true God, without a Teacher, and without a Law, the very servants of sin and satan, and without peace, for God did justly vex us for our sins; having lately, through his mercy, heard of the name of the True God, the name of his Son Christ Jesus, with the holy Ghost, the Comforter, three Persons, but one most Glorious God, whose name is JEHOVAH; wee do praise His

Glorious Greatness, and, in sorrow of our hearts, and shame of our faces, we do acknowledge and renounce our great and many sins, that we and our Fathers have lived in, do run unto him for mercy and pardon for Christ Jesus' sake; and we do this day, through the blessing of God upon us, and trusting to his gracious help, give up ourselves in this Covenant, Wee, our wives and children, to serve JEHOVAH: And we do this day chuse Jehovah to be our God in Christ Jesus, our Teacher, our Lawgiver in his Word, our King, our Judge, our Ruler by his magistrates and ministers; to fear God Himself, and to trust in Him alone for salvation, both of Soul and Body, in this present Life, and the Everlasting Life to come, through his mercy in Christ Jesus our Saviour and Redeemer, and by the might of his Holy Spirt, to whom, with the Father and Son, be all Glory everlasting, Amen."

Mr. Mayhew says, "I observed that the Indians, when they chose their Rulers, made choyce of such as were best approved for their godliness, and most likely to suppress sin, and encourage holiness. There was an Indian that was well approved for his Reformation, that was suspected to have told a plain Lye for his Gain; the business was brought to the public Meeting, and there it was notably sifted with zeal and good affection; but at length the Indian defending himself with great disdain and hatred of such evil, proved himself clear, and praised God for it."

He also relates the following anecdote:

"My Father and I were lately talking with an Indian who had not long before almost lost his life by a wound his Enemies gave him in a secret hidden way, the mark whereof he had upon him, and will carry it to his grave. This man understanding of a secret Plot that was to take away his Enemies life, told my Father and I, That he did freely forgive him for the sake of God, and did tell this Plot to us that the man's life might be preserved. This is a singular thing, and who among the Heathen will do so?"

Again: "*Myoxeo* also lately met with an Indian which came from the *Mayn*, (the main-land,) who was of some note among them. I heard that he told them of the great things of God, the sinfulness and folly of the Indians, the pardon of sin by Christ, and of a good life; and so they were both affected, that they continued this discourse two half nights and a day, until their strength was spent. He told him in particular how a Beleever did live above the world, that he did keep worldly things alwaies at his feet, (as he shewed him by a sign,) That when they were diminished or increased, it was neither the cause of his sorrow or joy, that he should stoop to regard them, but he stood upright with his heart Heavenward, and his whole desire was after God, and his joy in Him."

He says, "Within two or three weeks (1652) there came an Indian to me in business, and by the way he told me that some Indians had lately kept a day of Repentance to humble themselves before God in prayer, and that the word of God which one of them spake unto for their Instruction, was Psal. 66: 7. 'He ruleth by his Power forever, his eyes behold the nations, let not the rebellious exalt themselves.' I asked him what their end was in keeping such a day? He told me these six things. 1. 'They desired that God would slay the rebellion of their hearts. 2. That they might love God and one another. 3. That they might withstand the evil words of wicked men, and not be drawn back from God. 4. That they might be obedient to the good words and commands of their Rulers. 5. That they might have their sins done away by the Redemption of Jesus Christ. And Lastly, That they might walk in Christ's way.'"

In 1651, thirty Indian children were at school

which began in November, 1651. "They are apt to learn," says Mr. M., "and more and more are now sending in unto them."

"I was once," says Mr. M., "down towards the further end of the Island, and lodged at an Indian's house, who was accounted a great man among the Islanders, being the friend of the Sachem on the *Mayn.* At this man's house where I sate awhile, his son being about thirty years old, earnestly desired me, in his Language, to relate unto him some of the ancient stories of God. I then spent a great part of the night (in such discourse as I thought fittest for them) as I usually do when I lodg in their houses; what he then heard did much affect him. And shortly after he came and desired to joyn with the praying Indians to serve Jehovah." He was persecuted for this; but he told Mr. M. "That if they should stand with a sharp weapon against his breast, and tell him that they would kill him presently if he did not turn to them; but if he would, they would love him; yet he had rather lose his life than keep it on such terms."

A Powaw once told Mr. M. that after he had forsaken his powawing, and had begun to serve God, and to renounce his Imps, which he did in a public manner, the Imps still remained with him tormenting him, so that he could never be at rest, sleeping or waking. At a Lecture, sometime after, he asked Mr. M. this question: If a Powaw had his Imps gone from him, what he should have instead of them to preserve him? He was told if he believed in Christ "he should have the Spirit of Christ dwelling in him, which is a good and strong Spirit, and will so keep him safe, that all the Devils in Hell, and Powaws on earth, should not be able to do him any hurt; and that if he did set himself against his Imps by the strength of God, they should all flee away like muskeetooes." He replied, That soon after he had believed he was not troubled with any pain as formerly in his bed, nor dreadful visions of the night, but lay down with ease, slept quietly, waked in peace, and walked in safety; "for which he is very glad and praises God."

Mr. Mayhew also relates a fact, like the one already given respecting the feelings and conduct of the Christian Indians at the death and burial of their children. The case already mentioned, it will be remembered, occurred at Nonantum; this, at Martha's Vineyard. Mr. Mayhew says,

"I have observed the wise disposing hand of God in another providence of his. There have not, as I know, any man, woman, or child, died, of the meeting-Indians, since the meeting began, until now of late the Lord took away Hiacoomes, his child, which was about five days old. He was best able to make a good use of it, and to carry himself well in it, and so was his wife also; and truly they gave an excellent example in this also as they have in other things; here were no black faces for it as the manner of the Indians is, nor goods buried with it, nor hellish howlings over the dead, but a patient resigning of it to him that gave it. There were some English at the burial, and many Indians to whom I spake something of the Resurrection; and as we were going away, one of the Indians told me he was much refreshed in being freed from their old customes, as also to hear of the Resurrection of good men and their children to be with God."

One of the 'meeting-Indians' said that 'if all the world, the riches, plenty, and pleasures of it were presented without God, or God without all these, I would take God.'

Another said, 'If the greatest Sagamore in the land should take him in his arms, and proffer him his love, his riches and gifts, to turn him from his ways, he would not go with him from the way of God.'

One of them was heard, of his own accord,

in complaining against head knowledge and lip prayers, without heart holiness, loathing the condition of such a man, saying, I 'desire my heart may taste of the word of God, repent of my sins, and lean upon the Redemption of the Lord Jesus Christ.'

The following is a letter from a good man in this country to a friend in England, written about the year 1650.

'The best News I can write you from *New-England* is, the Lord is indeed converting the *Indians*, and for the refreshing of your heart, and the hearts of all the godly with you; I have sent you the Relation of one *Indian* of two yeares profession, that I took from his owne mouth by an Interpreter, because he cannot speak or understand one word of *English*.

THE FIRST QUESTION WAS;

Q. How did you come first to any sight of sinne?

A. His answer was, Before the Lord did ever bring any *English* to us, my Conscience was exceedingly troubled for sin, but after Mr. *Mayhew* came to preach, and had been here some time, one chiefe *Sagamore* did imbrace the Gospel, and I hearing of him, I went to him, and prayed him to speake something to me concerning God, and the more I did see of God, the more I did see my sinne, and I went away rejoycing, that I knew any thing of God, and also that I saw my sinne.

Q. I pray what hurt doe you see in sinne?

A. Sin, sayth he, is a continuall sicknesse in my heart.

Q. What further evill doe you see in sinne?

A. I see it to be a breach of all Gods Commandements.

Q. Doe you see any punishment due to man for sinne?

A. Yea, sayth he, I see a righteous punishment from God due to man for sinne, which shall be by the Devills in a place like unto fire (not that I speake of materiall fire, saith he) where man shall be for ever dying and never dye.

Q. Have you any hope to escape this punishment?

A. While I went on in the way of *Indianisme* I had no hope, but did verily believe I should goe to that place, but now I have a little hope, and hope I shall have more.

Q. By what meanes doe you look for any hope?

A. Sayth he, by the satisfaction of Christ.

I prayed the Interpreter, to tell him from mee that I would have him thinke much of the satisfaction of Christ, (and so he told him) I prayed him to returne mee his Answer.

A. I thanke him kindly for his good Counsell, it doth my heart good, sayd he, to heare any man speake of Christ.

Q. What would you thinke if the Lord should save you from misery?

A. If the Lord, said he, would save me from all the sinne that is in my heart, and from that misery, I should exceedingly love God, and, saith he, I should love a man that should doe mee any good, much more the Lord, if he should doe this for mee.

Q. Doe you thinke that God will doe you any good for any good that is in you?

A. Though I beleeve that God loves man that leaves his sinne, yet I beleeve it is for Christ's sake.

Q. Doe you see that at any time God doth answer your prayers?

A. Yea, sayth he, I take every thing as an Answer of prayer.

Q. But what speciall answer, have you taken notice of?

A. Once my wife being three dayes and three

nights in labour, I was resolved never to leave praying till she had deliverance, and at last God did it, and gave her a sonne, and I called his name *Returning*, because all the while I went on in *Indianisme* I was going from God, but now the Lord hath brought mee to him backe againe.

By this time Captaine *Gooking* came to us, and he asked him this Question:

Q. What he would thinke if he should finde more affliction and trouble in God's wayes, than he did in the way of Indianisme.

A. His answer was, when the Lord did first turne me to himselfe and his wayes, he stripped mee as bare as my skinne, and if the Lord should strip me as bare as my skinne againe, and so big *Saggamore* should come to mee, and say, I will give you so big Wampom, so big *Beaver*, and leave this way, and turne to us againe: I would say, take your riches to your selfe, I would never forsake God and his wayes againe.

This is a Relation taken by my selfe,

William French.'

There was a great fishing place at one of the falls of the Merrimack, where the Indians assembled in great numbers in the spring of the year, and Mr. Eliot went to meet them. He hired a Nashaway or Lancaster Indian to beat down a path for him from Roxbury through the woods, and to notch the trees that he might find his way through. His Church were concerned for his safety, on account of difficulties between two tribes through which his path lay. A Sachem with twenty men did escort for him, and the journey occupied three days. "It pleased God," he says, "to exercise us with such tedious rain and bad weather, that we were extreme wet, insomuch that I was not dry night nor day from the third day of the week to the sixth, but so traveled, and at night pull off my boots, wring my stockings, and on with them again. My horse was tired, so that I was forced to let him go without a rider and take one of the men's horses, which I took along with me. Yet God stept in and helped. I considered that word of God, 'Endure hardness as a good soldier of Jesus Christ.'"

It is not surprising that the questions proposed by the Indians should have excited so much interest among their English teachers, and the friends in England to whom they were communicated. Should similar questions be reported to us from a tribe of people among whom our missionaries had effected an entrance, we should feel that there was great promise of success among that people. It seems that many in England doubted the practicability of converting the North American savages. They were greatly surprised at the communications from Mr. Eliot; they saw that nothing was too hard for the Almighty, that Christ could save unto the uttermost, all who come unto God by him, that the Gospel was suited to the nature of man in every condition, that the story of the cross moved the heart of the savage as well as the civilized, and that Mr. Eliot's reflection after his first efforts in preaching at Nonantum was true, " That there is no need of miraculous or extraordinary gifts in seeking the salvation of the most depraved of the human family."

The Sudbury, Concord, Lancaster, Medford, and Dedham Indians had all in a few years received the Gospel from Nonantum. In visiting that interesting spot we cannot but say, " From you sounded out the word of the Lord."

A pious Indian from Martha's Vineyard visited the Indians of Merrimack weare. After he had been there, the Merrimack Indians stated this case to Mr. Eliot, for an explanation. 'If a strange Indian comes among us whom we never saw before, yet if he pray unto God we do exceedingly love him. But if my own brother, dwelling a great way off, come unto us, he not praying to God, though we love him, yet nothing so as we love that other stranger who doth pray unto God.'

CHAPTER VII.

Natick. The Indians build a bridge. Scenery of Charles River. The Arsenal at Watertown. Indian names. Mrs. Sigourney's Lines. Gov. Endicott's Letter. Proceedings preparatory to forming an Indian Church. Confessions of several Indians. Indian Catechism. Number in the Indian Church at Natick. Eliot's Indian Grammar. His Indian Bible. Remarks upon it. A copy sent to Charles II. Richard Baxter's remark. Further observations on the Indian Bible. 14 places of praying Indians, in 1660. Mr. Bancroft's testimony. Indian Youths at Harvard College.

We come now to another stage in the history of the Indian mission.

It has already been said that in 1650 Mr. Eliot obtained a grant of land for the Indians, for the purpose of building houses and organizing a town government. The place selected was called Natick, which means *a place of hills*. There the Indians began to build houses, each house having a piece of land attached to it for agriculture. One large building was erected to be the property of the town, the lower part to be used for a school-room and place of worship, the upper room to be a place of deposit for skins and articles of public property, with a bed for Mr. Eliot.

In one of his letters to friends in England, Mr. Eliot says,

"There is a great river which divideth between their planting grounds and dwelling place, through which they easily wade in summer, yet in the spring it is deep and unfit for daily passing over, especially of women and children." He proposed to the Indians that they should make a foot bridge over it, which was accordingly built, and was ninety feet long and nine feet high. When it was finished, Mr. Eliot called the Indians together, prayed, and gave thanks to God, and taught them out of a portion of Scripture. He then told them that as it had been hard and tedious labor in the water, if any of them desired wages for their work he would give it to them, yet considering the work was for their own use, if they should do all that labor in love, he should take it well and remember it.

They replied that they were far from desiring any wages for doing their own work, and on the contrary were thankful for their employment,—at which Mr. Eliot praised them for their readiness and ingenuity at such work. This bridge is said to have lasted longer than one which the English built about the same time at Dedham.

It would be interesting if we could identify

some of the favorite places of the Indians in this vicinity. It is pleasant to think that they were often grouped together at that most charming point where the Charles River bends round the arsenal at Watertown. No one who has stood on the bridge at that place on a summer morning when the mists were rising from the stream, or in the after part of the day, when the sun was in the right position over the curving parts of the stream to make their outlines brilliant as gold in the green meadow, can have failed to think that had such scenery occurred to him in Italy or Scotland, he would have found it celebrated in the works of the poet and painter. We have only to take journeys about home to find in the part of the country where we live, views and scenes both natural and historical of thrilling interest. It is easy to imagine the light canoe borne rapidly along the winding vales of the Charles River; we meet with Indian names in almost every village which is watered by that interesting stream, as well as in other places. Wrentham has its Nuckup hill; Norwich its Quenaboag and Shetucket river; Auburn its Boggachoog brook; Lancaster its Weshakum ponds; and Natick its Pegan plain.

The following lines by Mrs. Sigourney may appropriately be introduced here.

INDIAN NAMES.

"How can the red man be forgotten, while so many of our states and territories, bays, lakes and rivers, are indelibly stamped by names of their giving?"

Ye say, that all have passed away,
That noble race and brave,
That their light canoes have vanished
From off the crested wave;
That 'mid the forests where they roamed,
There rings no hunter's shout;
But their name is on their waters,
Ye may not wash it out.

'Tis where Ontario's billow,
Like Ocean's surge is curled,
Where strong Niagara's thunders wake
The echo of the world,
Where red Missouri bringeth
Rich tributes from the west,
And Rappahannock sweetly sleeps,
On green Virginia's breast.

Ye say their cone-like cabins,
That clustered o'er the vale,
Have fled away like withered leaves,
Before the autumn gale;
But their memory liveth on your hills,
Their baptism on your shore,
Your everlasting rivers speak
Their dialect of yore.

Old Massachusetts wears it
  Within her lordly crown,
And broad Ohio bears it
  Amid her young renown;
Connecticut hath wreathed it,
  Where her quiet foliage waves,
And bold Kentucky breathes it hoarse,
  Through all her ancient caves.

Wachuset hides its lingering voice,
  Within his rocky heart,
And Alleghany graves its tone
  Throughout his lofty chart;
Monadnock on his forehead hoar,
  Doth seal the sacred trust;
Your mountains build their monuments,
  Though ye destroy their dust.

The Society for Propagating the Gospel among the Indians of North America, an account of which will be found in the appendix to this volume, published a letter addressed to them by Governor Endicott, of Massachusetts. It is interesting as a testimony to the advancement which the Indians had made in religion and civilization, and as a specimen of the personal interest which good rulers in former times took in the promotion of the kingdom of Christ in the earth. The letter is here printed as it is written, with the Introduction by the Society:

"The next Letter you meet withall came from the present Governour of the *Massachusets*, directed to the President of our Corporation, and another of the Members thereof, which wee thought good to publish, that every Christian Reader may partake in the same consolation, wherewith he and we are comforted; and joyne with us in prayer to the Lord of the Harvest, that he would provide more Labourers to enter upon this soul-saving worke, and enlarge the hearts of all his people in this Nation towards the same."

"*Much honoured and beloved in the Lord Jesus:*

I Esteeme it not the least of God's mercies that hath stirred up the hearts of any of the people of God to be instrumentall in the inlarging of the Kingdome of his deare Sonne here amongst the Heathen *Indians*, which was one end of our comming hither, and it is not frustrated. It was prophesied of old, and now begins to be accomplished, *Psal.* 2: 8. Neither can I but acknowledge the unspeakable goodnesse of God that gives us favour in the sight of our Countreymen to helpe on with so large a hand of bounty, so glorious a work, provoked thereunto by your worthy selves, the chiefe Actors of so good a designe, let me (with leave) say confidently, you will never have cause to repent it; For the work is Gods and he doth owne it, the labour there hath been yours, and your Master will reward it. I think Religion and Conscience binde me to seek unto God for you, and to praise him with you, for what is already begun. The Foundation is laid, and such a one that I verily beleeve the gates of Hell shall never prevaile against. I doubt not but the building will goe on apace, which I hope will make glad the hearts of Thousands. Truly Gentlemen, had you been eare and eye-witnesses of what I heard and saw on a Lecture-day amongst them about three weeks since, you could not but be affected therewith as I was. To speak truly I could hardly refrain tears from very joy to see their diligent attention to the word first taught by one of the *Indians*, who before his Exercise prayed for the manner devoutly and reverently (the matter I not so well understanding) but it was with such reverence, zeale, good affection, and distinct utterance, that I could not but admire it; his Prayer was about a quarter of an houre or more, as we judged it; then he took his Text, and Mr. *Eliot* their Teacher told us that were *English*, the place (there were some Ministers and diverse other godly men there that attended me thither) his Text was in, *Matth.* 13: 44, 45, 46. [The kingdom of heaven is like unto treasure, &c. And to a merchant man, &c.] He continued in his Exercise full halfe an houre or more, as I judged it, his gravity and utterance was indeed very commendable; which being done Mr. *Eliot* taught in the *Indian* tongue about three quarters of an hour as neer as I could guesse; the *Indians* which were in number men and women neer about one hundred, seemed the most of them so to attend him, (the men especially) as if they would loose nothing of what was taught them, which reflected much upon some of our *English* hearers. After all there was a *Psalme* sung in the *Indian* tongue, and *Indian* meeter, but to an *English* tune, read by one of themselves, that the rest might follow, and he read it very distinctly without missing a word as we could judge, and the rest sang chearfully, and prettie tuneablie. I rid on purpose thither being distant from my dwelling about thirty eight, or forty miles, and truly I account it one of the best Journeyes I made these many years. Some few dayes after I desired Mr. *Eliot* briefly to write me the substance of the *Indians* Exercise, which when he went thither again, namely to *Naticke*, where the *Indians* dwell, and where the *Indian* taught, he read what he remembered of it first to their School-Master who is an *Indian*, and teacheth them and their Children to write, and I saw him write also in *English*, who doth it true and very legible, and asked him if it were right, and he said yea, also he read it unto others, and to the man himselfe, who also owned it. To tell you of their industry and ingenuitie in building of an house after the *English* manner, the hewing aad squaring of their tymber, the sawing of the boards themselves, and making of a Chimney in it, making of their ground-sells and wall-plates, and mortising, and letting in the studds into them artificially, there being but one *English* man a Carpenter to shew them, being but two dayes with them, is remarkeable. They have also built a Fort there with halfe trees cleft about eight or ten inches over, about ten or twelve foot high, besides what is intrencht in the ground, which is above a quarter of an acre of ground, as I judge. They have also built a foot bridge over *Charles* Rivers, with Groundsells and Spurres to uphold it against the strength of the Flood and Ice in Winter; it stood firme last Winter, and I think it will stand many Winters. They have made Drummes of their owne with heads and brases very neatly and artificially, all which shews they are industrious and ingenuous. And they intend to build a Water-Mill the next Summer, as I was told when I was with them. Some of them have learnt to mow grasse very well. I shall no further trouble you with any more Relation at this time concerning them. But a word or two further with your patience concerning other *Indians.* The work of God amongst the *Indians* at *Martins Vineyard*, is very hopefull and prosperous also. I mist of Mr. *Mayhew* their Teacher, who was lately at *Boston*, and therefore cannot give you a particular account thereof at this present time; yet I cannot but acquaint you what other motions there are touching other *Indians.* There came to us upon the 20th of this instant Moneth, at the Generall Court one *Pummakummim* Sachem of *Qunnubbágge*, dwelling amongst or neer to the *Narragansets*, who offered himselfe and his Men to worship God, and desired that some *English* may be sent from the *Massachusets* Government to plant his River, that thereby he may be partaker of Government, and may be instructed by the *English* to know God. We shall I hope take some care and course about it, and I hope we shall have more help to carry on that work also; For there are some Schollers amongst us who addict themselves to the study of the *Indian* Tongue. The Lord in mercy recompence it into your Bosomes, all that labour of love vouchsafed to the poor *Indians,* which are the hearty prayers, and earnest desire of, much honoured,

Boston the 27*th of*
the Eight. 1651.

Your loving Friend in all
service of Christ.
JOHN ENDECOTT."

The prudence and caution of Mr. Eliot in his proceedings with regard to the formation of a Church among the Indians are not a little remarkable. He says,

"In way of preparation of them thereunto, I did this Summer call forth sundry of them in the dayes of our public Assemblies in Gods Worship; sometimes on the Sabbath when I could be with them, and sometimes on Lecture daies, to make confession before the Lord of their former sins, and of their present knowledg of Christ, and experience of his Grace; which they solemnly doing, I wrote down their Confessions: which having done, and being in my own heart hopeful that there was among them fit matter for a Church, I did request all the Elders about us to hear them reade, that so they might give me advice what to do in this great and solemn business; which being done on a day appointed for the purpose, it pleased God to give their Confessions such acceptance in their hearts, as that they saw nothing to hinder their proceeding, to try how the Lord would appear therein. Whereupon, after a day of Fasting and Prayer among ourselves, to seek the Lord in that behalf, there was another day of Fasting and Prayer appointed, and publick notice thereof, and of the names of Indians were to confess, and enter into Covenant that day, was given to all the Churches about us, to seek the Lord yet further herein, and to make solemn Confessions of Christ his Truth and Grace, and further to try whether the Lord would vouchsafe such grace unto them, as to give them acceptance among the Saints, into the fellowship of Church-Estate, and enjoyment of those Ordinances which the Lord hath betrusted his Churches withal. That day was the thirteenth of the eighth month.

When the Assembly was met, the first part of the day was spent in Prayers unto God, and exercise in the Word of God; in which my self first and after that two of the Indians did Exercise; and so the time was spent till after ten or near eleven of the clock. Then addressing our selves unto the further work of the day, I first requested the reverend Elders (many being present) that they would ask them Questions touching the fundamental Points of Religion, that thereby they might have some tryal of their knowledg, and better that way, than if themselves should of themselves declare what they beleeve, or than if I should ask them Questions in these matters: After a little conference hereabout, it was concluded, That they should first make confession of their experience in the Lords Work upon their hearts, because in so doing, it is like something will be discerned of their knowledg in the Doctrines of Religion: and if after those Confessions there should yet be cause to inquire further touching any Point of Religion it might be fitly done at last. Whereupon we so proceeded, and called them forth in order to make confession. It was moved in the Assembly by Reverend Mr. *Wilson*, that their former Confessions also, as well as these which they made at present, might be read unto the Assembly, because it was evident that they were daunted much, to speak before so great and grave an Assembly as that was, but time did not permit it so to be then: yet now in my writing of their Confessions I will take that course, that so it may appear what encouragement there was to proceed so far as we did; and that such as may reade these their Confessions, may the better discern of the reality of the Grace of Christ in them."

He afterwards says,

"In the year 52 I perceiving the grace of God in sundry of them, and some poor measure of fitnesse (as I was perswaded) for the enjoyment of Church-fellowship, and Ordinances of Jesus Christ, I moved in that matter, according as I have in the Narration thereof, briefly declared. In the year 53 I moved not that way, for these Reasons.

I having sent their Confessions to be published in *England*, I did much desire to hear what acceptance the Lord gave unto them, in the hearts of his people there, who daily labour at the Throne of grace, and by other expressions of their loves, for an holy birth of this work of the Lord, to the praise of Christ, and the inlargement of his Kingdome. As also my desire was, that by such Books as might be sent hither, the knowledge of their Confessions might be spread here, unto the better and fuller satisfaction of many, then the transacting thereof in the presence of some could doe. These Books came by the latter Ships (as I remember) that were bound for *New England*, and were but newly out when they set saile, and therefore I had not that answer that year, which my soule desired, though something I had which gave encouragement, and was a tast of what I have more fully heard from severall this year, praised be the Lord.

Besides there fell a great damping and discouragement upon us by a jealousie too deeply apprehended, though utterly groundlesse, *viz.* That even these praying *Indians* were in a conspiracy with others, and with the *Dutch*, to doe mischief to the *English.* In which matter, though the ruling part of the People looked otherwise upon them, yet it was no season for me to stir or move in this matter, when the waters were so troubled. This businesse needeth a calmer season, and I shall account it a favour of God when ever he shall please to cause his face to shine upon us in it. Yet this ¶ did the last year, after the Books had been come a season, there being a great meeting at *Boston*, from other Colonies as well as our owne, and the Commissioners being there, I thought it necessary to take that opportunity to prepare and open the way in a readinesse against this present year, by making this Proposition unto them; namely, *That they having now seen their confessions, if upon further triall of them in point of knowledge, they be found to have a competent measure of understanding in the fundumentall points of*

Religion; and also, if there be due testimony of their conversation, that they walke in a Christian manner according to their light, so that Religion is to be seen in their lives; whether then it be according to God, and acceptable to his people, that they be called up unto Church estate? Unto which I had I blesse the Lord, a generall approbation.

Accordingly this year 54 I moved the Elders, that they would give me advice and assistance in this great businesse, and that they would at a fit season examine the *Indians* in point of their knowledge, because we found by the former triall, that a day will be too little (if the Lord please to call them on to Church-fellowship) to examine them in points of Knowledge, and hear their Confessions, and guide them into the holy Covenant of the Lord. Seeing all these things are to be transacted in a strange language, and by Interpreters, and with such a people as they be in these their first beginnings. But if they would spend a day on purpose to examine them in their knowledge there would be so much the more liberty to doe it fully and throughly, (as such a work ought to be) as also when they may be called to gather into Church-Communion, it may suffice that some one of them should make a Doctrinall Confession before the Lord and his people, as the rule of faith which they build upon, the rest attesting their consent unto the same: And themselves (the Elders I mean, if the Lord so far assist the *Indians*, as to give them satisfaction) might testifie that upon Examination they have found a competency of knowledge in them to inable them unto such a work and state. And thus the work might be much shortned, and more comfortably expedited in one day. I found no unreadinesse in the Elders to further this work.

They concluded to attend the work, and for severall Reasons advised that the place should be at *Roxbury*, and not at *Natick*, and that the *Indians* should be called thither, the time they left to me to appoint, in such a season as wherein the Elders may be at best liberty from other publick occasions. The time appointed was the 13 of the 4 moneth; meanwhile I dispatched Letters unto such as had knowledge in the Tongue, requesting that they would come and help in interpretation, or attest unto the truth of my Interpretations. I sent also for my Brother *Mayhu*, who accordingly came, and brought an Interpreter with him. Others whom I had desired, came not. I informed the *Indians* of this appointment, and of the end it was appointed for, which they therefore called, and still doe, when they have occasion to speak of it *Natootomuhteáe kesuk, A day of asking Questions, or, A day of Examination.* I advised' them to prepare for it, and to pray earnestly about it, that they might be accepted among Gods people, if it were the will of God.

It pleased God so to guide, that there was a publick Fast of all the Churches, betwixt this our appointment, and the accomplishment thereof: which day they kept, as the Churches did, and this businesse of theirs was a Principall matter in their Prayers."

It will be useful, as well as interesting, to give some of the "Confessions of Indians" which were made and considered in preparation for their entering into the Church state.

CONFESSION OF TOTHERSWAMP.

"Before I prayed unto God, the English, when I came unto their houses, often said unto me, Pray to God; but I having many friends who loved me, and I loved them, and they cared not for praying to God, and therefore I did not: But I thought in my heart, that if my friends should die, and I live, I then would pray to God; soon after, God so wrought, that they did almost all die, few of them left; and then my heart feared, and I thought, that now I will pray unto God, and yet I was ashamed to pray; and if I eat and did not pray, I was ashamed of that also; so that I had a double shame upon me: Then you came unto us, and taught us, and said unto us, *Pray unto God;* and after that, my heart grew strong, and I was no more ashamed to pray, but I did take up praying to God; yet at first I did not think of God and eternal Life, but only that the English should love me and I loved them: But after I came to learn what sin was, by the Commandments of God, and then I saw all my sins, lust, gaming, &c. (he named more.) You taught, That Christ knoweth all our hearts, and seeth what is in them, if humility, or anger, or evil thoughts, Christ seeth all that is in the heart; then my heart feared greatly, because God was angry for all my sins; yea, now my heart is full of evil thoughts, and my heart runs away from God, therefore my heart feareth and mourneth. Every day I see sin in my heart; one man brought sin into the World, and I am full of that sin, and I break Gods Word every day. I see I deserve not pardon, for the first mans sinning; I can do no good, for I am like the Devil, nothing but evil thoughts, and words, and works. I have lost all likeness to God, and goodness, and therefore every day I sin against

God, and I deserve death and damnation: The first man brought sin first, and I do every day add to that sin, more sins; but Christ hath done for us all righteousness, and died for us because of our sins, and Christ teacheth us, That if we cast away our sins, and trust in Christ, then God will pardon all our sins; this I beleeve Christ hath done, I can do no righteousness, but Christ hath done it for me; this I beleeve, and therefore I do hope for pardon. When I first heard the Commandments, I then took up praying to God and cast off sin. Again, When I heard, and understood Redemption by Christ, then I beleeved Jesus Christ to take away my sins: every Commandment taught me sin, and my duty to God. When you ask me why do I love God? I answer, Because he giveth me all outward blessings, as food, clothing, children, all gifts of strength, speech, hearing; especially that he giveth us a Minister to teach us, and giveth us Government; and my heart feareth lest Government should reprove me; but the greatest mercy of all is Christ, to give us pardon and life."

"TOTHERSWAMP

The Confession which he made on the Fast day before the great Assembly was as followeth:

I Confess in the presence of the Lord, before I prayed, many were my sins, not one good word did I speak, not one good thought did I think, not one good action did I doe: I did act all sins, and full was my heart of evil thoughts; when the English did tell me of God, I cared not for it, I thought it enough if they loved me: I had many friends that loved me, and I thought if they died I would pray to God: and afterward it so came to pass; then was my heart ashamed, to pray I was ashamed, and if I prayed not, I was ashamed; a double shame was upon me: when God by you taught us, very much ashamed was my heart; then you taught us that Christ knoweth all our hearts: therefore truly he saw my thoughts, and I had thought, if my kindred should die I would pray to God; therfore they dying, I must now pray to God; and therefore my heart feared, for I thought Christ knew my thoughts: then I heard you teach, *The first man God made was named* Adam, *& God made a Covenant with him, Do and live, thou and thy Children; if thou do not thou must die, thou* *and thy Children:* And we are Children of *Adam* poor sinners, therefore we all have sinned, for we have broke Gods Covenant, therefore evil is my heart, therefore God is very angry with me, we sin against him every day; but this great mercy God hath given us, he hath given us his only Son, and promiseth, That whosoever beleeveth in Christ shall be saved: for Christ hath dyed for us in our stead, for our sins, and he hath done for us all the words of God, for I can do no good act, only Christ can, and only Christ hath done all for us; Christ hath deserved pardon for us, and risen again, he hath ascended to God, and doth ever pray for us; therefore all Beleevers Souls shall goe to Heaven to Christ. But when I heard that word of Christ, Christ said *Repent and Beleeve*, and Christ seeth *who Repenteth*, then I said, dark and weak is my Soul, and I am one in darkness, I am a very sinful man, and now I pray to Christ for life. Hearing you teach that Word that the Scribes and Pharisees said *Why do thy Disciples break the Tradition of the Fathers?* Christ answered, *Why do you make void the Commandments of God?* Then my heart feared that I do so, when I teach the Indians, because I cannot teach them right, and thereby make the word of God vain. Again, Christ said *If the blind lead the blind they will both fall into the ditch;* Therefore I feared that I am one blind, and when I teach other Indians I shal caus them to fall into the ditch. This is the love of God to me, that he giveth me all mercy in this world, and for them al I am thankfull; but I confess I deserve Hell; I cannot deliver my self, but I give my Soul and my Flesh to Christ, and I trust my soul with him for he is my Redeemer, and I desire to call upon him while I live.

This was his Confession which ended, Mr. *Allin* further demanded of him this Question, How he found his heart, now in the matter of Repentance?

His answer was; I am ashamed of all my sins, my heart is broken for them and melteth in me, I am angry with my self for my sins, and I pray to Christ to take away my sins, and I desire that they may be pardoned.

But it was desired that further Question might be forborn, lest time would be wanting to here them all speak."

The following is the Confession of Waban, (or the wind,) the man in whose wigwam Mr. Eliot preached to the Indians in the beginning of his ministry among them, and who, from Mr. Eliot's text, "Prophesy unto the wind," &c., supposed that the message of God was specially directed to himself.

CONFESSION OF WABAN.

"Before I heard of God, and before the English came into this Country, many evil things my heart did work, many thoughts I had in my heart; I wished for riches, I wished to be a witch, I wished to be a Sachem; and many such other evils were in my heart: Then when the English came, still my heart did the same things; when the English taught me of God (I coming to their Houses) I would go out of their doors, and many years I knew nothing; when the English taught me I was angry with them: But a little while agoe after the great sikness, I considered what the English do; and I had some desire to do as they do; and after that I began to work as they work; and then I wondered how the English come to be so strong to labor; then I thought I shall quickly die, and I feared lest I should die before I prayed to God; then I thought, if I prayed to God in our Language, whether could God understand my prayers in our Language; therefore I did ask Mr. *Jackson*, and Mr. *Mahu,* If God understood prayers in our Language? They answered me God doth understand all Languages in the World. But I do not know how to confess, and little do I know of Christ; I fear I shall not beleeve a great while, and very slowly; I do not know what grace is in my heart, there is but little good in me; but this I know, That Christ hath kept all Gods Commandements for us, and that Christ doth know all our hearts; and now I desire to repent of all my sins: I neither have done, nor can do the Commandements of the Lord, but I am ashamed of all I do, and I do repent of all my sins, even of all that I do know of: I desire that I may be converted from all my sins, and that I might beleeve in Christ, and I desire him; I dislike my sins, yet I do not truly pray to God in my heart: no matter for good words, all is the true heart; and this day I do not so much desire good words, as throughly to open my heart: I confess I can do nothing, but deserve damnation; only Christ can help me and do for me. But I have nothing to say for my self that is good; I judg that I am a sinner, and cannot repent, but Christ hath deserved pardon for us."

'This Confession being not so satisfactory as was desired, Mr. *Wilson* testified, that he spake these latter expressions with tears, which I observed not, because I attended to writing; but I gave this testimony of him, That his conversation was without offence to the English, so far as I knew, and among the Indians it was exemplar: his gift is not so much in expressing himself this way, but in other respects useful and eminent; it being demanded in what respects, I answered to this purpose, That his gift lay in Ruling, Judging of Cases, wherein he is patient, constant, and prudent, insomuch that he is much respected among them, for they have chosen him a Ruler of Fifty, and he Ruleth well according to his measure. It was further said, they thought he had been a great drawer on to Religion; I replyed, so he was in his way, and did prevail with many; and so it rested.

"CONFESSION OF WILLIAM, OF SUDBURY.

I CONFESS that before I prayed, I committed all manner of sins, and served many gods: when the English came first, I going to their houses, they spake to me of your God, but when I heard of God, my heart hated it; but when they said the Devil was my god, I was angry, because I was proud: when I came to their houses I hated to hear of God, I loved lust in my own house and not God, I loved to pray to many gods. Five years ago, I going to English houses, and they speaking of God, I did a little like of it, yet when I went again to my own house, I did all manner of sins, and in my heart I did act all sins though I would not be seen by man. Then going to your house, I more desired to hear of God; and my heart said, I will pray to God so long as I live: then I went to the Minister Mr. *Browns* house, and told him I would pray as long as I lived: but he said I did not say it from my heart, and I beleeve it. When *Waban* spake to me that I should pray to God, I did so. But I had greatly sinned against God, and had not beleeved the Word but was proud: but then I was angry with my self, and loathed my self, and thought God will not forgive me my sins. For when I had been abroad in the woods I would be very angry, and would lye unto men, and I could not find the way how to be a good man: then I beleeved your teaching, That when good men die, the Angels carry their souls to God; but evil men dying, they go to Hell, and perish for ever. I thought this a true saying, and I promised to God, to pray to God as long as I live. I had a little grief in my heart five years ago for my sins: but many were my prides; sometime I was angry with my self, and pityed my self; but I thought God would not pardon such a proud heart as mine is: I beleeve that Christ would have me to forsake my anger; I beleeve that Christ hath redeemed us, and I am glad to hear those words of God; and I desire that I might do al the good waies of God, and that I might truly pray unto God: I do now want Graces, and these Christ only teacheth us, and only Christ hath wrought our redemption, and he procureth our pardon for all our sins; and I beleeve that when beleevers dy, Gods Angels carry them to Heaven; but I want faith to beleeve the Word of God, and to open my Eyes, and to help me to cast away all sins; and Christ hath deserved for me eternall life: I have deserved nothing my self: Christ hath deserved, all, and giveth me faith to beleeve it."

"CONFESSION OF MONEQUASSUN, THE SCHOOLMASTER.

I Confess my sorrow for all my sins against God, and before men: When I first heard instruction, I beleeved not, but laughed at it, and scorned praying to God; afterward, when we were taught at *Cohannet* (that is the place where he lived) I still hated praying, and I did think of running away, because I cared not for praying to God; but afterwards, because I loved to dwell at that place, I would not leave the place, and therfore I thought I will pray to God, because I would still stay at that place, therefore I prayed not for the love of God, but for love of the place I lived in; after that I desired a little to learn the Catechisme on the Lecture daies, and I did learn the ten Commandements, and after that, all the points in the Catechisme; yet afterwards I cast them all away again, then was my heart filled with folly, and my sins great sins, afterwards by hearing, I began to fear, because of my many sins, lest the wise men should come to know them, and punish me for them; and then again I thought of running away because of my many sins: But after that I thought I would pray rightly to God, and cast away my sins; then I saw my hypocricy, because I did ask some questions, but did not do that which I knew: afterward I considered of my question, and thought I would pray to God, and would consider of some other Question, and I asked this Question, *How should I get Wisdom?* and the Answer to it did a little turn my heart from sin, to seek after God; and I then considered that the Word of God was good; then I prayed to God because of the Word of God. The next Lecture day you taught that word of God, *If any man lack Wisdom, let him ask it of God, who giveth freely to them that ask him, and upbraideth no man, James*, 1: 5. Then again a little my heart was turned after God, the Word also said, *Repent, mourn, and beleeve in Jesus Christ:* this also helped me on. Then you taught, *That he that beleeveth not Christ, and repenteth not of sin, they are foolish and wicked; and because they beleeve not, they shall perish:* then I thought my self a fool, because I beleeved not Christ, but sinned every day, and after I heard the Word greatly broke the Word. But afterward I heard this promise of God, *Who ever repenteth and beleeveth in Christ, God will forgive him all his sins, he shall not perish;* then I thought, that as yet, I do not repent, and beleeve in Christ: then I prayed to God, because of this his Promise; and then I prayed to God, for God and for Christ his sake: after that again I did a little break the Word of Christ. And then I heard some other words of God, which shewed me my sins, and my breakings of Gods word; and sometimes I thought God and Christ would forgive me, because of the promise to them that beleeve in Christ, and repent of sin, I thought I did that which God spake in the Promise. Then being called to confess, to prepare to make a Church at *Natick*, I loved *Cohannet;* but after hearing this instruction, *That we should not only be Hearers, but Doers of the Word*, then my heart did fear. And afterward hearing that in *Matthew*, Christ saw two brethren mending their Nets, he said, *Follow me and I will make you Fishers of men*, presently they followed Christ; and when I heard this, I feared, because I was not willing to follow Christ to *Natick;* they followed Christ at his Word, but I did not, for now Christ saith to us, *follow Me:* then I was much troubled, and considered of this Word of God. Afterward I heard another word, the blind men cried after Christ and said, *Have mercy on us thou Son of David*, but after they came to Christ he called them, and asked them, *What shall I do for you?* they said, *Lord open our eyes;* then Christ had pity on them, and opened their eyes, and they followed Christ; when I heard this, my heart was troubled, then I prayed to God and Christ, to open mine eyes, and if Christ open my eyes, then I shall rejoyce to follow Christ: then I considered of both these Scriptures, and I a little saw that I must follow Christ. And now my heart desireth to make confession of what I know of God, and of my self, and of Christ: I beleeve that there is only one God, and that he made and ruleth all the World, and that he the Lord, giveth us al good things: I know that God giveth every day all good mercies, life, and health, and all; I have not one good thing, but God it is that giveth it me, I beleeve that God at first made man like God, holy, wise, righteous; but the first man sinned, for God promised him, *If thou do my Commandements, thou shalt live, and thy Children; but if thou sin, thou shalt die, thou and thy children;* this Covenant God made with the first man. But the first man did not do the Commandements of God he did break Gods Word, he beleeved Satan; and now I am full of sin, because the first man brought sin; dayly I am full of sin in my heart: I do not dayly rejoyce in Repentance, because Satan worketh dayly in my heart, and opposeth Repentance, and all good Works; day and night my heart is full of sin. I beleeve that Jesus Christ was born of the *Virgin Mary;* God promised her she should bear a Son, and his Name should be J E S U S, because he shall deliver his people from their sins: And when Christ came to preach, he said, *Repent, because the Kingdom of Heaven is at hand;* again Christ taught, *Except ye repent and become as a little child, ye shall not enter into the Kingdom of Heaven;* therefore humble your selves like one of these little children, and great shall be your Kingdom in Heaven. Again Christ said, *Come unto me all ye that are weary and heavy laden with sin, and I will give you rest: take up my Cross and Yoak, learn of me for I am meek, and ye shall find rest to your souls, for my yoak is easie and burden light:* these are the Words of Christ and I know Christ he is good, but my works are evil: Christ his words are good, but I am not humble; but if we be humble and beleeving in Christ, he pardons all our sins. I now desire to beleeve in Jesus Christ, because of the word of Christ, that I may be converted and become as a little Child. I confess my sins before God, and before Jesus Christ this day; now I desire all my sins may be pardoned; I now desire repentance in my heart, and ever to beleeve in Christ; now I lift up my heart to Christ, and trust him with it, because I beleeve Christ died for us, for all our sins, and deserved for us eternal life in Heaven, and deserved pardon for all our sins. And now I give my soul to Christ because he hath redeemed: I do greatly love, and like repentance in my heart, and I love to beleeve in Jesus Christ, and my heart is broken by repentance: al these things I do like wel of, that they may be in my heart, but because Christ hath all these to give, I ask them of him that he may give me repentance, and faith in Christ, and therefore I pray and beseech Christ dayly for repentance and faith; and other good waies I beg of Christ dayly to give me: and I pray to Christ for al these gifts and graces to put them in my heart: and now I greatly thank Christ for all these good gifts which he hath given me. I know not any thing, nor can do any thing that is a good work: even my heart is dark dayly in what I should do, and my soul dyeth because of my sins, and therefore I give my soul to Christ, because my soul is dead in sin, and dayly doth commit sin; in my heart I sin, and all the members of my body are sinful. I beleeve Jesus Christ is ascended to Heaven through the clouds, and he will come again from Heaven: Many saw Christ go up to Heaven, and the Angels said, even so he will come again to judg all the world; and therefore I beleeve Gods promise, That all men shall rise again when Christ cometh again, then all shall rise, and all their souls comes again because Christ is trusted with them, and keeps their souls, therefore I desire my sins may be pardoned;

and I beleeve in Christ; and ever so long as I live, I will pray to God, and do all the good waies he commandeth."

"CONFESSIONS OF ROBIN SPEENE.

I was ashamed because you taught to pray to God, and I did not take it up; I see God is angry with me for all my sins, and he hath afflicted me by the death of three of my children, and I fear God is still ăngry, because great are my sins, and I fear lest my children be not gone to Heaven, because I am a great sinner, yet one of my children prayed to God before it died, and therefore my heart rejoyceth in that. I remember my Pawwawing [for he was a *Pawwaw*] my lust, my gaming, and all my sins; I know them by the Commandements of God, and God heareth and seeth them all; I cannot deliver my self from sin, therefore I do need Christ, because of all my sins, I desire pardon, and I beleeve that God calls all to come to Christ, and that he delivereth us from sin."

"*His Second Confession.*

I have found out one word more: great are my sins, and I do not know how to repent, nor do I know the evil of my sins; only this one word, now I confess I want Christ, this day I want him; I do not truly beleeve nor repent: I see my sin, and I need Christ, but I desire now to be redeemed: and I now ask you this Question *What is Redemption?* "I answered him, " by shewing him our estate by Nature, and " desert, the price which Christ paid for us, and " how it is to be applied to every particular " person; which done, he proceeded in his confession thus: I yet cannot tell whether God hath pardoned my sins, I forget the word of God; but this I desire, that my sins may be pardoned, but my heart is foolish, and a great part of the Word stayeth not in my heart strongly. I desire to cast all my sins out of my heart: but I remember my sins, that I may get them pardoned, I think God doth not yet hear my prayers in this, because I cannot keep the Word of God, only I desire to hear the Word, and that God would hear me."

"*His Third Confession.*

One word more I cal to mind, Great is my sin! this saith my heart, I have found this sin, when I first heard you teach, that all the world from the rising to the sitting Sun should pray to God, I then wondered at it, and thought, I being a great sinner, how shal I pray to God; and when I saw many come to the Meeting, I wondred at it: But now I do not wonder at that work of God, and therefore I think that I do now greatly sin: and now I desire again to wonder at Gods Works, and I desire to rejoyce in Gods good waies. Now I am much ashamed, and fear because I have deserved eternal wrath by my sins: my heart is evil, my heart doth contrary to God: and this I desire, that I may be redeemed, for I cannot help my self, but only Jesus Christ hath done al this for me, and I deserve no good, but I beleeve Christ hath deserved all for us: and I give my self unto Christ, that he may save me, because he knoweth eternal life, and can give it; I cannot give it to my self, therefore I need Jesus Christ, my heart is full of evil thoughts; and Christ only can keep my soul from them, because he hath paid for my deliverance from them."

"CONFESSION OF ANTONY.

Another who made his Confession is named *Antony*, upon whom the Lord was pleased the last Winter to lay an heavy stroke; for he and another Indian being at work sawing of

Board, and finishing the Peece, they laid it so short, and the Rowl not so stedfast, insomuch that this man being in the Pit directing to lay the Piece, and the other above ordering thereof, it slipped down into the Pit upon this mans head, brake his neather Chap in two, and cracked his Skull, insomuch that he was taken up half dead, and almost strangled with blood; and being the last day of the week at night I had no word until the Sabbath day, then I presently sent a Chyrurgion, who took a discreet order with him; and God so blessed his indeavors, as that he is now well again, blessed be the Lord: and whereas I did fear that such a blow in their Labor might discourage them from Labor, I have found it by Gods blessing otherwise; yea this man hath performed a great part of the sawing of our Meeting-House, and is now sawing upon the School-house, and his recovery is an establishment of them to go on; yea, and God blessed this blow, to help on the Work of Grace in his soul; as you shall see in his Confession, which followeth.

Before I prayed to God I alwaies committed sin, but I do not know all my sins, I know but a little of the sins I have committed, therefore I thought I could not pray to God, because I knew not al my sins before I prayed to God, and since I heard of praying to God: formerly when the English did bid me pray unto God I hated it, and would go out of their houses, when they spake of such things to me. I had no delight to hear any thing of Gods Word, but in every thing I sinned; in my speeches I sinned, and every day I broke the Commands of God. After I heard of praying to God; that *Waban* and my two brothers prayed to God, yet then I desired it not, but did think of running away; yet I feared if I did run away some wicked men would kill me, but I did not fear God. After when you said unto me, pray, my heart thought, I will pray; yet again I thought, I cannot pray with my heart, and no matter for praying with words only: but when I did pray, I saw more of my sins; yet I did but only see them, I could not be aware of them, but still I did commit them: and after I prayed to God, I was still full of lust, and then a little I feared. Sometimes I was sick, and then I thought God was angry, and then I saw that I did commit all sins: then one of my brothers died, and then my heart was broken, and after him another friend, and again my heart was broken: and yet after all this I broke my praying to God, and put away God, and then I thought I shall never pray to God: but after this I was afraid of the Lord, because I alwaies broke my praying to God and then my heart said, God doth not hear my prayer. When I was sick, and recovered again, I thought then that God was merciful unto me. Hearing that word of God, *If you hear the Word of God, and be forgetful hearers, you sin against God;* then I thought God will not pardon such a sinner as I, who dayly did so, and broke my praying to God. When I heard the Commandements, I desired to learn them, and other points of Catechism, but my desires were but small, and I soon lost it, because I did not desire to beleeve: then sometimes I feared Gods anger because of al my sins; I heard the Word and understood only this word, *All you that hear this day, it may be you shall quickly die,* and then I quickly saw that God was very angry with me. Then God brake my head, and by that I saw Gods anger; and then I thought that the true God in Heaven is angry with me for my sin, even for al my sins, which every day I live, I do. When I was almost dead, some body bid me now beleeve, because it may be I shal quickly die, and I thought I did beleeve, but I did not know right beleeving in Christ: then I prayed unto God to restore my health. Then I beleeved that word, *That we must shortly appear before Jesus Christ;* then I did greatly fear lest if I beleeved not, I should perish for ever. When I was neer death, I prayed unto God, *Oh Lord give me life, and I will pray to God so long as I live*, and I said, *I will give my self, soul, and body to Christ:* after this, God gave me health, and then I thought, truly, God in Heaven is merciful; then I much grieved, that I knew so little of Gods Word. And now sometimes I am angry, and then I fear because I know God seeth it; and I fear, because I promised God when I was almost dead, that if he giveth me life, I will pray so long as I live; I fear lest I should break this promise to God. Now I desire the pardon of all my sins, and I beg faith in Christ, and I desire to live unto God, so long as I live; I cannot myself get pardon, but I dayly commit sin, and break Gods Word, but I look to Christ for pardon."

" CONFESSION OF EPHRAIM.

All the daies I have lived, I have been in a poor foolish condition, I cannot tell all my sins, all my great sins, I do not see them. When I first heard of praying to God, I could not sleep quietly, I was so troubled, ever I thought I would forsake the place because of praying to God, my life hath been like as if I had been a mad man. Last yeer I thought I would leave all my sins, yet I see I do not leave off sinning to this day; I now think I shall never be able to forsake my sins. I think sometimes the Word of God is false, yet I see there is no giving over that I might follow sin, I must pray to God; I do not truly in my heart repent, and I think that God wil not forgive me my sins: every day my heart sinneth, and how will Christ forgive such an one? I pray but outwardly with my mouth, not with my heart; I cannot of my self obtain pardon of my sins: I cannot tell all the sins that I have done if I should tell you an whol day together: I do every morning desire that my sins may be pardoned by Jesus Christ; this my heart saith, but yet I fear I cannot forsake my sins, because I cannot see all my sins: I hear, That if we repent and beleeve in Christ, all our sins shall be pardoned, therefore I desire to leave off my sins.

This poor Publican was the last which made his Confession before I read them unto the Elders, and the last of them I shall now publish. I will shut up these Confessions with the Confession (if I may so call it) or rather with the Expression, and manifestation of faith, by two little Infants, of two yeers old, and upward, under three yeers of age when they died and departed out of this world.

The Story is this,

THIS Spring, in the beginning of the yeer, 1652, the Lord was pleased to afflict sundry of our praying Indians with that grievous disease of the Bloody-Flux, whereof some with great torments in their bowels died; among which were two little Children of the age above-said, and at that time both in one house, being together taken with that disease. The first of these Children in the extremities of its torments, lay crying to God in these words, *God and Jesus Christ, God and Jesus Christ help me;* and when they gave it any thing to eat, it would greedily take it (as it is usual at the approach of death) but first it would cry to God, *Oh God and Jesus Christ, bless it,* and then it would take it: and in this manner it lay calling upon God and Jesus Christ untill it died: The mother of this Child also died of that disease, at that time. The Father of the Child told me this story, with great wonderment at the grace of God, in teaching his Child so to call upon God. The name of the

Father is *Nishohkou*, whose Confession you have before.

Three or four daies after, another Child in the same house, sick of the same disease, was (by a divine hand doubtless) sensible of the approach of death, (an unusual thing at that age) and called to its Father, and said, *Father, I am going to God*, several times repeating it, *I am going to God.* The mother (as other mothers use to do) had made for the Child a little Basket, a little Spoon, and a little Tray: these things the Child was wont to be greatly delighted withal (as all Children will) therefore in the extremity of the torments, they set those things before it, a little to divert the mind, and cheer the spirit: but now, the child takes the Basket, and puts it away, and said, *I will leave my Basket behind me, for I am going to God, I will leave my Spoon and Tray behind me* (putting them away) *for I am going to God:* and with these kind of expressions, the same night finished its course, and died.

The Father of this child is named *Robin Speen*, whose Confessions you have before, and in one of them he maketh mention of this child that died in Faith. When he related this story to me, he said, He could not tell whether the sorrow for the death of his child, or the joy for its faith were greater, when it died.

These Examples are a testimony, That they teach their children the knowledg and fear of God, whom they now call upon; and also that the Spirit of God co-worketh with their instructions, who teacheth by man, more than man is able to do."

Mr. Eliot says, 'I have now finished all that I purpose to publish at this time; the Lord give them Acceptance in the hearts of his Saints, to engage them the more to pray for them; and Oh! that their judgings of themselves, and breathings after Christ, might move others (that have more means than they have, but as yet regard it not) to do the like, and much more abundantly.'

A meeting of the Elders of the Churches was requested by Mr. Eliot, as before stated, to give advice in view of these Confessions, and upon further personal examination of some of the Indians, as to the next step to be taken in organizing the Indian Church. But Mr. E. says,

"There fell out a very great discouragement a little before the time, which might have been a scandall unto them, and I doubt not but Satan intended it so; but the Lord improved it to stir up faith and Prayer, and so turned it another way: Thus it was. Three of the unsound sort of such as are among them that pray unto God, who are hemmed in by Relations, and other means, to doe that which their hearts love not, and whose Vices Satan improveth to scandalize and reproach the better sort withall; while many, and some good people are too ready to say they are all alike. I say three of them had gotten severall quarts of strong water, (which sundry out of a greedy desire of a little gaine, are too ready to sell unto them, to the offence and grief of the better sort of *Indians*, and of the godly English too)* and with these Liquors, did not onely make themselves drunk, but got a Child of eleven years of age, the Son of *Tote-swamp*, whom his Father had sent for a little Corne and Fish to that place near *Watertowne* where they were. Unto this Child they first gave too spoonfuls of Strong-water, which was more then his head could bear; and another of them put a Bottle, or such like Vessel to his mouth, and caused him to drink till he was very drunk; and then one of them domineered, and said, *Now we will see whether your Father will punish us for drunkennesse* (for he is a Ruler among them) *seeing you are drunk with us for*

* See the Memorial of Mr. Eliot to the General Court, on this subject, Appendix L.

company; and in this case lay the Child abroad all night. They also fought, and had been severall times Punished formerly for Drunkennesse.

When *Toteswamp* heard of this, it was a great shame and breaking of heart unto him, and he knew not what to doe. The rest of the Rulers with him considered of the matter, they found a complication of many sins together.

1 The sin of Drunkennesse, and that after many former Punishments for the same.

2 A willful making of the Child drunk, and exposing him to danger also.

3 A degree of reproaching the Rulers.

4 Fighting.

Word was brought to me of it, a little before I took Horse to goe to *Natick* to keep the Sabbath with them, being about ten dayes before the appointed Meeting. The Tidings sunk my spirit extreamly, I did judge it to be the greatest frowne of God that ever I met withall in the work, I could read nothing in it but displeasure, I began to doubt about our intended work: I knew not what to doe, the blacknesse of the sins, and the Persons reflected on, made my very heart faile me: For one of the offendors (though least in the offence) was he that hath been my Interpreter, whom I have used in Translating a good part of the Holy Scriptures; and in that respect I saw much of Satans venome, and in God I saw displeasure. For this and some other acts of Apostacy at this time, I had thoughts of casting him off from that work, yet now the Lord hath found a way to humble him. But his Apostacy at this time was a great Triall, and I did lay him by for that day of our Examination, I used another in his room. Thus Satan aimed at me in this their miscarrying; and *Toteswamp* is a Principall man in the work, as you shall have occasion to see anon God-willing.

By some occasion our Ruling Elder and I being together, I opened the case unto him, and the Lord guided him to speak some gracious words of encouragement unto me, by which the Lord did relieve my spirit; and so I committed the matter and issue unto the Lord, to doe what pleased him, and in so doing my soul was quiet in the Lord. I went on my journey being the 6 day of the week; when I came at *Natick*, the Rulers had then a Court about it. Soon after I came there, the Rulers came to me with a Question about this matter, they related the whole businesse unto me, with much trouble and grief.

Then *Toteswamp* spake to this purpose, *I am greatly grieved about these things, and now God tryeth me whether I love Christ or my Child best. They say, They will try me; but I say,*

God will try me. Christ saith, He that loveth father, or mother, or wife, or Child, better than me, is not worthy of me. Christ saith, I must correct my Child, if I should refuse to doe that, I should not love Christ. God bid Abraham kill his Son, Abraham loved God, and therefore he would have done it, had not God with-held him. God saith to me, onely punish your Child, and how can I love God, if I should refuse to doe that? These things he spake in more words, and much affection, and not with dry eyes: Nor could I refraine from teares to hear him. When it was said, The Child was not so guilty of the sin, as those that made him drunk; he said, *That he was guilty of sin, in that he feared not sin, and in that he did not believe his counsells that he had often given him, to take heed of evill company; but he had believed Satan and sinners more then him, therefore he needed to be punished.* After other such like discourse, the Rulers left me, and went unto their businesse, which they were about before I came, which they did bring unto this conclusion, and judgement, They judged the three men to sit in the stocks a good space of time, and thence to be brought to the whipping-Post, & have each of them twenty lashes. The boy to be put in the stocks a little while, and the next day his father was to whip him in the School, before the Children there; all which Judgement was executed. When they came to be whipt, the Constable fetcht them one after another to the Tree (which they make use of instead of a Post) where they all received their Punishments: which done, the Rulers spake thus, one of them said, *The Punishments for sin are the Commandements of God, and the worke of God, and his end was, to doe them good, and bring them to repentance.* And upon that ground he did in more words exhort them to repentance, and amendment of life. When he had done, another spake unto them to this purpose, *You are taught in Catechisme, that the wages of sin are all miseries and calamities in this life, and also death and eternall damnation in hell. Now you feele some smart as the fruit of your sin, and this is to bring you to repentance, that so you may escape the rest.* And in more words he exhorted them to repentance. When he had done, another spake to this purpose, *Heare all yee people* (turning himselfe to the People who stood round about, I think not lesse then two hundred, small and great) *this is the Commandement of the Lord, that thus it should be done unto sinners; and therefore let all take warning by this, that you commit not such sins, least you incur these Punishments.*

And with more words he exhorted the People. Others of the Rulers spake also, but some things spoken I understood not, and some things slipt from me: But these which I have related remained with me.

When I returned to *Roxbury*, I related these things to our Elder, to whom I had before related the sin, and my grief: who was much affected to hear it, and magnified God. He said also, That their sin was but a Transient act, which had no Rule, and would vanish. But these Judgements were an ordinance of God, and would remaine, and doe more good every way, then their sin could doe hurt, telling me what cause I had to be thankfull for such an issue: Which I therefore relate, because the Lord did speak to my heart, in this exigent, by his words."

This difficulty being thus settled, the time came for the meeting of the Elders. Mr. Eliot observes,

"When the assembly was met for Examination of the *Indians*, and ordered, I declared the end and Reason of this Meeting, and therefore declared, That any one, in due order, might have liberty to propound any Questions for their satisfaction. Likewise, I requested the Assembly, That if any one doubted of the Interpretations that should be given of their answers, that they would Propound their doubt, and they should have the words scanned and tryed by the Interpreters, that so all things may be done most clearly. For my desire was to be true to Christ, to their soules, and to the Churches: And the trying out of any of their Answers by the Interpreters, would tend to the satisfaction of such as doubt, as it fell out in one Answer which they gave; the Question was, *How they knew the Scriptures to be the word of God?* The finall Answer was, Because they did find that it did change their hearts, and wrought in them wisedome and humility. This Answer being Interpreted to the Assembly, my Brother *Mahu* doubted, especially of the word [*Hohpoóonk*] signifying *Humility*, it was scanned by the Interpreters, and proved to be right, and he rested satisfied therein. I was purposed my selfe to have written the Elders Questions, and the *Indians* Answers, but I was so imployed in propounding to the *Indians* the Elders Questions, and in returning the *Indians* Answers, as that it was not possible for me to write unlesse I had caused the Assembly to stay upon it, which had not been fitting; therefore seeing Mr. *Walton* writing, I did request him to write the Questions and Answers, and help me with a Copy of them, which I thank him, he did, a Copy whereof I herewith send to be inserted in this place, on which, this only I will animadvert, That the Elders in wisdome thought it not fit to ask them in Catechisticall method strictly, in which way Children might Answer. But that they might try whether they understood what they said, they traversed up and downe in Questions of Religion, as here you see.

POSTCRIPT.

LET the Reader take notice, That these questions were not propounded all to one man, but to sundry, which is the reason that sometime the same Questions are propounded againe and againe. Also the number Examined were about eight, namely, so many as might be first called forth to enter into Church-Covenant, if the Lord give opportunity."

We have a Catechism, entitled " The Examination of the Indians at Roxbury, the 13th day of the 4th month, 1654. The following are some of the questions and answers.

Q. Have not some Indians many Gods?

A. They have many Gods.

Q. How doe you know these Gods are no Gods.

A. Before the English came we knew not but that they were Gods, but since they came we know they are no Gods :

Q. How doe you know the word of God is Gods word ?

A. I believe the word that you teach us, was spoken of God.

Q. Why doe you believe it ?

A. Therefore I believe it to be the word of God, because when we learn it, it teacheth our hearts to be wise and humble.

Q. Whether are not your sins, and the temptations of *Hobbomak* more strong since, then before you prayed to God ?

A. Before I prayed to God, I knew not what Satans temptations were.

Q. Doe you know now ?

A. Now I have heard what Satans temptations are.

Q. What is a temptation of the Devill in your heart, doe you understand what it is ?

A. Within my heart there are Hypocrisies, which doe not appear without.

Q. Whether doe not you find this a principall temptation from the wickednesse of your heart, to drive you away from Christ, and not to believe the gracious Promises in Jesus Christ? Or whether when you find wickednesse in your heart, you are not tempted that you cannot believe?

A. My heart doth strongly desire to goe on in sin, but this is a strong temptation, but Faith is the work of Jesus Christ.

Q. What doe you believe about the immortality of the soule, and resurrection of the body? doth the soule dye when the body dyeth?

A. I believe, when the body of a good man dyeth, the Angels carry his soule to heaven, when a wicked man dyeth, the Devills carry his soule to hell.

Q. How long shall they be in that state?

A. Untill Christ cometh to Judgement.

Q. When Christ cometh to judge the world, what then shall become of them?

A. The dead bodies of all men shall rise againe.

Q. Whether shall they ever dye any more?

A. Good men shall never dye any more.

Q. Whether doe you believe that these very bodies of ours shall rise againe?

A. This body which rots in the earth, this very body, God maketh it new.

Q. Who is Jesus Christ?

A. Jesus Christ is the Son of God, yet borne man, and so both God and man.

Q. Why was Christ Jesus a man?

A. That he might dye for us.

Q. Why is Christ Jesus God?

A. That his death might be of great value.

Q. Why doe you say, Christ Jesus was a man that he might dye, doe onely men dye?

A. He dyed for our sins.

Q. What reason or justice is there, that Christ should dye for our sins?

A. God made all the world, and man sinned, therefore it was necessary Christ should dye to carry men up to Heaven. God hath given unto us his Son Jesus Christ, because of our sins.

The Question being put to another for further Answer, his Answer was, *That God so loved the world, that he gave his onely begotten Son, that whosoever believeth in him should not perish, but have everlasting life.*

Q. When you heare that *Adam* by his sin deserved eternall death, and when you hear of the grace of God sending Jesus to save you, which of these break your heart most?

A. Pardon of sin goeth deepest."

With regard to the formation of the church, one writer says;

"This great and solemne work of calling up

these poor Indians unto that Gospel light and beauty of visible Church-cstate, having now passed through a second Tryall: In the former whereof, they expressed what experience they had found of Gods grace in their hearts, turning them from dead works, to seek after the living God, and salvation in our Saviour Jesus Christ. In this second they have in some measure declared how far the Lord hath let in the light of the good knowledge of God into their soules, and what tast they have of the Principles of Religion, and doctrine of salvation. Now the Question remaineth, *What shall we further doe? And when shall they enjoy the Ordinances of Jesus Christ in Church-estate?*

"The work is very solemne, and the Question needeth a solemne Answer. It is a great matter to betrust those with the holy priviledges of Gods house, upon which the name of Christ is so much called, who have so little knowledge and experience in the wayes of Christ, so newly come out of that great depth of darknesse, and wild course of life; in such danger of polluting and defiling the name of Christ among their barbarous Friends and Countrey-men; and under so many doubts and jealousies of many people; and having not yet stood in the wayes of Christ so long, as to give sufficient proof and experience of their stedfastnesse in their new begun profession. Being also the first Church gathered among them, it is like to be a pattern and president of after proceedings, even unto following Generations. Hence it is very needfull that this proceeding of ours at first, be with all care and wearinesse guided, for the most effectuall advancement of the holinesse and honour of Jesus Christ among them.

"Upon such like grounds as these, though I and some others know more of the sincerity of some of them, than others doe, and are better satisfied with them: Yet because I may be in a temptation on that hand, I am well content to make slow hast in this matter, remembring that word of God, *Lay hands suddenly on no man.* Gods works among men doe usually goe on slowly, and he that goeth slowly, doth usually goe most surely, especially when he goeth by counsell. *Sat cito si sat bene,** the greater proof we have of them, the better approbation they may obtain at last. Besides, we having had one publick meeting about them already this summer, it will be difficult to compasse another, for we have many other great occasions, which may hinder the same, and it is an hard matter to get Interpreters together to attend such a work, they living so remote. The dayes also will

* Fast enough, if well enough.

soon grow short, and the nights cold, which will be an hindrance in the attendance unto the accomplishment of that work, which will most fitly be done at *Natick.*

"But above all other Reasons this is greatest, that they living in sundry Towns and places remote from each other, and labourers few to take care of them, it is necessary that some of themselves should be trained up, and peculiarly instructed, unto whom the care of ruling and ordering of them in the affaires of Gods house may be committed, in the absence of such as look after their instruction. So that this is now the thing we desire to attend, for the comfort of our little *Sister that hath no breasts,* that such may be trained up, and prepared, unto whom the charge of the rest may be committed in the Lord. And upon this ground we make the slower hast to accomplish this work among them. Mean while I hope the Commissioners will afford some encouragement for the furtherance of the instruction of some of the most godly and able among them, who may be in a speciall manner helpfull unto the rest, in due order and season.

"And thus have I briefly set down our present state in respect of our Ecclesiasticall proceedings. I beg the prayers of the good people of the Lord, to be particularly present at the Throne of Grace, in these matters, according as you have hereby a particular Information how our condition is. And for me also, who am the most unfit in humane reason for such a work as this, but my soule desireth to depend and live upon the Lord Jesus, and fetch all help, grace, mercy, assistance, and supply from him. And herein I doe improve his faithfull Covenant and Promises, and in perticular, the Lord doth cause my soule to live upon that word of his, *Psal.* 37 : 3, 4, 5, 6, 7, wherein I have food, rayment, and all necessaries for my selfe and children (whom I have dedicated unto the Lord, to serve him in this work of his, if he will please to accept of them) and this supply I live upon in these rich words of gracious Promise, *verse* 3. *Trust in the Lord, and doe good, dwell in the Land, and verily thou shalt be fed.*

Herein also I find supply of grace to believe the conversion of these poor Indians, & that not only in this present season, in what I doe already see, but in the future also, further then by mine eye or reason I can see. Which supply of grace, I live upon in those words of his gracious Promise, which I apply and improve in this particular respect, *verse* 4. *Delight thy-*

selfe also in the Lord, and he shall give thee the desires of thy heart.

"Herein also I find supply of grace to believe, that they shall be in Gods season, which is the fittest, brought into Church Estate; faith fetching this particular blessing out of the rich Fountaine of those gracious words of Promise, *Commit thy way unto the Lord, trust also in him, and he shall bring it to passe.*

"Herein also my soule is strengthened and quieted, to stay upon the Lord, and to be supported against all suspitious jealousies, hard speeches, and unkindnesses of men, touching the sincerity and reality of this work, and about my carriage of matters, and supply herein. Which grace my soule receiveth by a particular improvement of that rich treasury of the Promise in these words, *verse* 6. *And he shall bring forth thy righteousnesse as the light, and thy judgement as the noon day.* And herein likewise I find supply of grace, to wait patiently for the Lords time, when year after year, and time after time, I meet with disappointments. Which grace I receive from the commanding force of that gracious Promise, *verse* 7. *Rest in the Lord, and wait patiently for him, fret not thy selfe,* either for one cause, or another. Thus I live, and thus I labor, here I have supply, and here is my hope, I beg the help of prayers, that I may still so live and labour in the Lords work, and that I may so live and dye."

In 1670, the number of men and women in full communion at Natick, was between forty and fifty, and more than three hundred and fifty had renounced their savage practices and open sins, and gave heed to the instructions of the Gospel.

Their meetings were notified by the drum. In their assemblies they were attentive and reverent. A native teacher commenced worship with prayer, and the English Christains assisted in the business of instruction. There, as at other times, and in other places among civilized people God poured out his Spirit upon the young. Several cases of hopeful piety in young children are mentioned. The most interesting of them have already been given.

Mr. Eliot having made a grammar of the Indian tongue, and a catechism, was proceeding with his Indian Bible. In 1649, he said it was his earnest wish to translate some parts of the Scriptures for the Indians. He probably labored at this work, at intervals, for twelve years, and he was at least forty-five years of age when he began it.

It should be remembered that this work, unlike the same employment of our foreign missionaries at their first arrival at new stations, was wholly in addition to his labors as Pastor of another people,—the congregation at Roxbury. It was of no direct use to him in his ministerial work, any farther than investigation and study is always profitable to the mind. It was a labor superadded to the cares and toil of his pastoral and ministerial office.

A man who has a taste for languages is generally repaid for the labor of acquiring them, by the stores of learning which they contain. Cato learned Greek at the age of eighty, and the literary world mention it to his praise. But here is a man learning a language which has no literature. No tragic or heroic muse had left her inspired strains in it. No beautiful old ballads or legendary songs repaid his labor,—no Canterbury Tales, or Children in the Wood, or Chevy Chase, or Fairy Queen, hymns of devotion, nor martial songs; the language could only whoop and powaw; the great word, gathering subjunctives and adjuncts into itself, like a crowded wigwam, was savagely ignorant of the graces, or the concise, vigorous expressions of some barbarous tongues, and Eliot's researches into it were like digging, as the Plymouth settlers did, into the mounds for corn, and finding nothing but skulls. But nothing could repress the ardor of his benevolent mind. He was determined that the Indians should have the word of God in their own tongue, and the work drew near to its accomplishment.

But how could it ever be printed? His slender salary could not pay for it; the planters could not subscribe an adequate sum. In a letter to England in 1651, he says, with much sorrow, "I have no hope to see the Bible printed in my days."

The Society for Propagating the Gospel came to his help.* In September, 1661, the New Testament in the Indian tongue was published at Cambridge. Three years after this, the Old Testament was added, and the whole Bible, with a Catechism and the Psalms of David in metre, was thus given to the Aborigines of this desert, in their own tongue, in forty years after the settlement of the country.

This was the first Bible printed on this Continent. It was printed at Cambridge, by Samuel Green and Marmaduke Johnson. A copy handsomely bound, was sent to King Charles II., and the Rev. Richard Baxter says of it, "Such a work and fruit of a plantation was never be-

* See Appendix E.

fore presented unto a king." Two hundred copies, in plain and strong leather, were immediately put in circulation for the use of the Indians. An angel would almost have exchanged his heavenly joy for the happiness of Eliot, when he visited Natick, and saw the Bible in the hands of the natives. Like old Jacob, strengthening himself upon his dying bed, he might then have said, "I have waited for thy salvation, O Lord;" or, like Simeon, "Now, Lord, lettest thou thy servant depart in peace, for mine eyes have seen thy salvation."

Douglass, in his History of America,* says, "Mr. Eliot with immense labor translated and printed our Bible into Indian. It was done with a good pious design, but it must be reckoned among the *otiosorum hominum negotia*, (works of men of leisure). It was done in the Natick (Nipmuck) language. Of the Naticks, at present, there are not twenty families subsisting, and scarce any of these can read. *Cui bono?*" (To what profit?)

Those who know how far Mr. Eliot was from being a man of leisure, will smile at the suggestion that the translation of the Bible into the Indian tongue was the work of an idle amateur. The disappearance of the race for whom this translation was designed, so unexpected,

*I. 172, Note. 1745.

and indeed so contrary to the fond hopes of our forefathers, is very far from showing the futility of Mr. Eliot's pious labor. Many of the Indians were made wise unto eternal life by the translated Bible. The good which it accomplished was more than an equivalent for the labor which it cost.

Cotton Mather says, "Behold, ye Americans, the greatest honour that ever you were partakers of. This Bible was printed here at our Cambridge, and it is the only Bible that ever was printed in all America, from the very foundation of the world. The whole translation he writ with but one pen; which pen, had it not been lost, would have certainly deserved a richer case than was bestowed upon that pen with which Holland writ his translation of Plutarch. *

---

*Mag. II, 511. *Philemon Holland.* See Rees' Encyc., Aiken's Biog. Mem. of Medicine. He was the *translator general* of his age, a man of incredible industry. In Fuller's Worthies of England we learn that Holland, having written several translations with one pen, made the following stanza:

"With one sole pen I writ this book,
Made of a gray goose quill;
A pen it was when I it took,
And a pen I leave it still."

A familiar story is told of Gibbon, in writing the "Decline and Fall," and that he presented the pen to the Duchess of Devonshire, who honored it with a silver case. These stories are probably fabu-

The New Testament was published first, and then the whole Bible, Primers, Grammars, Psalters, Catechisms, The Practice of Piety, Baxter's Call, Shepard's sincere Convert and Sound Believer, soon appeared in the Indian tongue, from the pen of Mr. Eliot.

By this time there were fourteen places of praying Indians under the care of Mr. Eliot, and about eleven hundred souls who were apparently converted. Natick, Stoughton, Grafton, Tewksbury, Hopkinton, Oxford, Dudley, Woodstock (three villages), Uxbridge and Marlboro', all had communities of praying Indians.

Mr. Bancroft, in his History of the United States,* says, "No pains were spared to teach them to read and write, and in a short time a larger proportion of the Massachusetts Indians could do so, than recently of the inhabitants of Russia." The Indians of Cape Cod, Martha's Vineyard, and Nantucket, amounting to about twenty-nine hundred, also were, by the labors of the Mayhews and others, partly evangelized. Mr. Eliot says, in 1673, that there were six churches gathered among the Indians, one at

lous. The contrivances which these men must have used to make one pen, or even one quill, do so much work, would deserve the appellation above quoted from Douglass, "otiosorum hominum negotia,"—or, the notions of men who had plenty of leisure.

* II. 94.

Natick, one at Grafton, one at Marshpee, two at Martha's Vineyard, and one at Nantucket. All these had religious teachers devoted exclusively to them, except the church at Natick, of which Mr. Eliot says, "In modesty they stand off, because they say that so long as I live, there is no need." They could not be prevailed upon to have another teacher even with the advantages of his entire devotion to them, while Mr. Eliot was alive.

Cotton Mather says,* "The number of preachers to the Indians increases apace. At Martha's Vineyard, the old Mr. Mayhew and several of his sons, or grand-sons, have done very worthily for the souls of the Indians; there were fifteen years ago by computation about fifteen hundred souls of their ministry, upon that one island. In Connecticut, the holy and acute Mr. Fitch has made noble essays towards the conversion of the Indians; but I think the sinner he has to deal withal, being an obstinate infidel, gives unhappy rumor as to the successes of his ministry. And godly Mr. Pierson has, if I mistake not, deserved well in that colony upon the same account. In Massachusetts we see at this day the pious Mr. Gookin, the gracious Mr.

* Magnalia I, 516.—See Appendix G.

Peter Thacher, the well accomplished and industrious Mr. Grindal Rawson, all of them hard at work, to turn these poor creatures from darkness to light, and from Satan unto God. In Plymouth we have the most active Mr. Samuel Treat laying out himself to save this generation, and there is one Mr. Tupper, who uses his laudable endeavours for the instruction of them.

"'Tis my relation to him * that causes me to defer unto the last place the mention of Mr. John Cotton, who hath addressed the Indians in their own language with some dexterity. He hired an Indian after the rate of twelve pence per day, for fifty days, to teach him the Indian tongue; but his knavish tutor having received his whole pay too soon, ran away before twenty days were out; however, in this time he had profited so far that he could quickly preach unto the natives."

Two Indians from Martha's Vineyard were entered at Harvard College. Their names were Joel and Caleb. Joel was lost on his voyage from Boston to Nantucket just before taking his degree. Caleb was graduated, but soon died of

---

* Cotton Mather's mother was the daughter of Mr. Cotton.

consumption at Charlestown. His name now stands on the College Catalogue in this form: "1665, Caleb Cheesehahteaumuck, Indus." He composed a Latin and Greek Elegy on the death of an eminent minister, and subscribed them, "Cheesehahteaumuck, Senior Sophista."

CHAPTER VII.

Disturbance of Missionary efforts. Philip's War. Removal of the Indians to Deer Isle. Return. Conclusion of the History of Missionary efforts among the Indians of this neighborhood. Reflections.

Civilization and the influence of the Gospel, however, had their limits. The Narraganset Indians, situated between the Connecticut and Plymouth Colonies, refused the Gospel, and the benevolent intentions of the English. King Philip, the famous warrior of Mount Hope, (now Bristol) whose name was terrible to our forefathers, scorned the doctrines of the cross. Mr. Eliot once had an interview with him, explained the way of salvation, and exhorted him to repent. The Indian chieftain rose, took hold of Mr. Eliot's button, and told him, that he cared no more for his Gospel than he did for that button.

The Indians under Philip were growing jealous of English encroachments upon their hunting fields. Petty depredations were made by the Indians upon the English settlements, then followed a summons to court, which, in process of time, became exceedingly annoying to proud, untamed savages. They had bartered their lands for English implements and toys; the tools and the toys were gone, and the savage could not be satisfied to abide by a paper, call it treaty, bond, or contract, on which he had scratched his mark. He sighed for his old domains; the waves of civilization were coming round him like a flood; his people were artfully crowded by the English into narrow inlets between the settlements, that they might be watched on all sides.

King Philip was summoned to Court in 1674, for some offence committed by his tribe. The informer was murdered by the angry savages. The murderers were hanged by the English. The massacre of eight or nine of the English at Swansey was the consequence. Philip wept when he heard that the blood of a white man had been shed. The Colonists began to arm, and a universal panic prevailed. The superstition of those days added much to the general terror. Signs in the heavens were reported to have been seen, a scalp on the disc of the moon in an eclipse; an Indian bow was imprinted on the sky. Troops of horses were heard rushing through the air. The horrors of an Indian war made their faces pale and their hearts faint. The scenes at Bloody Brook, the burning of Lancaster, Medfield, Brookfield, Weymouth, Groton, Marlborough, the ambushments rising on the congregation as they returned from public worship, the massacre of wives and children at home, and the scalping of husbands and brothers in the field, roused the colonies of Plymouth, Massachusetts, and Connecticut to an exterminating war.

It is easy to see that the communities of praying Indians could not escape the influence of the general excitement against the Indians. Some of them were accused, justly or unjustly, of favoring the designs of the enemy. The Colonists were all the time afraid that the instinctive love of war and carnage in the Indian bosom would break through the restraints of religion, and that all which had been done for the Indians would be only a qualification of them as more successful traitors and expert butchers.

On the other hand, King Philip was jealous of the praying Indians. He used every means of persuasion and fear to enlist them on his side. Their situation was trying in the extreme. In the excited state of mind which an Indian war created among the English, a war on the part of the savages of stratagem, and treachery, it was natural that the Christian Indians should be trusted and feared. Some of them enlisted with the English and did good service, and some deserted to Philip.

In 1675, a number of the Christian Indians were brought to Boston on a charge of being concerned in a murder at Lancaster. Mr. Eliot and his friends interposed to save them, and succeeded in showing that the accusation was false and malicious. In so doing, they incurred the popular resentment, and were suspected and accused of bad motives and treasonable conduct.

The feelings of the people were now so unreasonable that the worst consequences to the praying Indians were apprehended. In this state of things the General Court, as a means of protection to themselves and to the Indians, passed an order that the Natick Indians should be removed to Deer Island, in Boston harbor, between four and five miles from shore. They came to the place called the Pines, near Cambridge, on Charles River, and were thence conveyed by water to Deer Island. Mr. Eliot met them at the Pines, and endeavored to soothe and cheer them. He was then seventy years old. One might question whether he or the Indians suffered most in their removal.

A party of Indians had fired a barn at Chelmsford. The English imputed it to the praying Indians at Tewksbury. A party of the English went to their wigwams, called them out and shot one lad, and wounded several women and children. The murderers were tried, but the jury were overawed by the public sentiment and cleared them. The Tewksbury Indians fled into the wilderness; messengers were sent to them inviting them to return, but they gave this answer: We are not sorry for what we leave behind, but we are sorry that the English have driven us from praying to God, and from our leader. We did begin to understand a little of praying to God. When the winter season came, their sufferings forced them back to their wigwams, and the English endeavored in various ways to atone for the injuries they had suffered.

The Stoughton Indians, for some suspicion, were also removed to Deer Island, and the whole number there amounted to five hundred. Mr. Eliot and his friends visited them, and found them patient and meek, exhibiting the true influence of the Gospel in a satisfactory degree. But they were exposed to want and suffering of various kinds. The ill-treatment of other communities of Indians followed in rapid succession, and it was in vain that they sought in moments of contention, to repair the injuries which they had inflicted. One party of Indians, for example, had been taken by a Narraganset Sachem, and had escaped, and were wandering in the woods, when an English scouting party met them, taking from them, among other things, a pewter cup which Mr. Eliot had given them for their communion service, and which they had kept and carried with them with the reverence of a Jew for his sacred vessels of gold and silver. This party were also carried to Deer Island.

Philip, the terror of the English Colonies on this continent, was finally destroyed. The war subsiding, the Deer Island Indians, with the permission of the General Court, and by the funds of the society in England for propagating the Gospel, were removed to Cambridge, and were permitted to choose their places of settlement. Some of them went to the various falls of Charles River, some to Brush Hill in Milton, some settled at Nonantum, and many of them went to Natick.

But the efforts to Christianize the Indians were never resumed with the interest and zeal which were formerly felt. On the part of the English, there was conscience of wrong, and on the part of the Indians a remembrance of injustice, and thus a breach was made between them which was never healed. Some of the Indians had been made slaves. King Philip's wife and son had been sold in the West Indies.* Mr. Eliot followed with his prayers and efforts those of his Christian Indians who had been sold into bondage. He wrote to the celebrated and honorable Robert Boyle to use his efforts in redeeming some who had been left at Tangier.

By various means the praying towns had been reduced in 1684, to four. The tribes have dwindled and finally disappeared, till a few years since one poor hut in Natick, inhabited by a family of Indian and Negro blood, and the gravestone of Daniel Takawambait in the stone wall, were the most prominent of the memorials which they have left behind them. Fragments of their language are imperishably associated with many places and scenes throughout the land. The rural retreat, the new town, the gallant ship, are emulous of their names; while the tavern sign, the bank note, the omnibus, and the tobacconist, grace themselves with their faces and implements. The New England poet,

---

* See Appendix, M.

historian, and orator, draw thrilling incidents from Mount Hope and Bloody Brook, and the Christian and the philanthropist will enshrine the names of Nonantum and Natick. Westward and still westward, the New England tribes have receded. Civilization has had more repulsion and injury for the savage than Christianity has been able to overcome. There is a law of progress in the affairs of nations expressed in the prophetic language of the patriarch Noah; "God shall enlarge Japhet, and he shall dwell in the tents of Shem." The savage retreats before the civilized man, and while we mourn over the ruin of individual tribes, we cannot but stand in awe of that resistless measure of God's providence by which he is forcing the Caucasian race to fill the earth, and suffering uncivilized nations to melt away like the snow in spring.

But that same vigorous faith which brought the Pilgrims here as missionaries to the Indians, has followed the red man in his wanderings over this vast continent. The names of David Brainard, Samuel Kirkland, and Gideon Blackburn, are identified with the history of Indian missions. The American Board has pursued the work of evangelizing them with much success. The history of the Cherokees, the mountaineers of America, is of itself a tale of romantic and thrilling interest. The sketches of the present North American Indians by Mr. Catlin, in his valuable work, show that a large field for missionary effort on this continent is yet spread before the American churches.

When the workmen were digging for the foundation of some new houses at the corner of Tremont and Boylston streets, in Boston, several years ago, they found the skeleton of an Indian. He had been buried on his side, reclining on his arm, and was found in that posture. Christian faith and hope, mingled with a little fancy, would fain lead us to hail this incident as a sign that the Indian race are not yet recumbent in hopeless degradation; that though seemingly buried in the great wilderness, they are buried in the posture of rising. Many interesting recollections, and our natural feelings towards an oppressed people, make us wish that this was more than fancy, and, as the Indian on the seal of the Massachusetts colony had a passage of Scripture proceeding from his mouth, Come over and help us, would we gladly put another passage into the mouth of that resurrection Indian above mentioned, making him say, with prophetic ecstasy, as he looks towards Nonantum and surveys the scenes of his ancient, and apparently lost race, " Thy dead men shall live, together with my dead body shall they arise ; awake and sing, ye that dwell in dust, for thy dew is as the dew of herbs, and the earth shall cast out her dead."

CHAPTER VIII.

Mr. Eliot's avowal of republicanism, and his retraction of it. His connection with the controversy about Mrs. Hutchinson. Richard Baxter's Testimony about Mr. Eliot. Roman Catholics instructing the Indians. Mrs. Eliot. Close of Mr. Eliot's life. Conclusion.

Two events in the life of Mr. Eliot must necessarily be noticed in giving a complete account of him. One is the publication and subsequent retraction of a book called the Christian Commonwealth, and the other is his connection with the controversy raised by that notorious woman, Mrs. Anne Hutchinson.

Mr. Eliot wrote a book about the year 1650, called the Christian Commonwealth. It was carried to England in manuscript and printed. In 1660, the Governor and Council of Massachusetts condemned this book as being "full of seditious principles and notions in relation to all established governments in the Christian world, especially against the government established in their native country."

Mr. Eliot wrote an acknowledgment of error as the author of the book, and presented his recantation to the General Court. He speaks in it of Cromwell and his friends as "the late innovators" in the government of Great Britain, and of the monarchy as restored under Charles II., "as not only a lawful but eminent form of government." The book was suppressed, and Mr. Eliot's recantation was published through the colony.

This incident has been considered as reflecting on Mr. Eliot's character for discretion, or for decision. The book does not survive in this country to speak for itself. The facts in the case seem to be that during the success of Cromwell, Mr. Eliot composed his book in accordance with what seemed to be the tendency in England towards a settled republican form of government. But upon the restoration of Charles II., the provincial government of Massachusetts felt in duty bound to show their allegiance to the crown by protesting against the sentiments of a book which favored republicanism. How often it is the case that success is regarded as settling the question of right. Had Cromwell's plan succeeded, the Massachusetts government would not have felt obliged to condemn Mr. Eliot's book. We may perhaps reflect upon him for not maintaining and defending the principles of his book; but to have done so would have been treason, seeing that monarchy had again become the established form of government in the mother country. Mr. Eliot, perhaps, felt that it was right for him to find reasons for that permanent change in the government of Great Britain which in the providence of God seemed to be at hand. When the event proved otherwise than he expected, loyalty being then so much a part of religion, and "the powers" in the government of the mother country being, according to the received opinions of Christians, and like all other powers "that be," "ordained of God," it was a question with Mr. Eliot between decision and boldness, amounting to a treasonable spirit, and submission to constituted authority. The ill success of Cromwell no doubt made Eliot think that he had misinterpreted the purposes of God. Men are apt to feel and reason in this manner. If a colony, or province, or a number of men make insurrection, and succeed in overthrowing the government, men call it a revolution, and the independence of the new state or nation is acknowledged. If they do not succeed, the attempt is called a plot, conspiracy, insurrection, and the actors who in the event of success would have been "the fathers of their country," "the founders of a nation," are gibbeted by their generation, and regarded as traitors by the next, and by the world. While a revolution is pending, a man may say many things as an observer and theorizer, which, when events contradict them, he will do his best to retract, or cover up. It cannot be wondered at, that, amid the enthusiasm which attended the Restoration, and the implicit submission of the Colonial government to the restored king, and influenced by the loyal spirit of his times, Mr. Eliot should have deemed it a Christian duty to confess and retract that which the providence of God seemed to indicate was an error. He was not prepared to lift up a standard against the government of Great Britain; the appeal which Cromwell and his friends had made to the God of nations and of battles, had not been answered in his favor, and Mr. Eliot was meek enough to yield submission to that which, in the circumstances, seemed to be a Christian obligation. What should he have done? Had he still believed that Cromwell was the anointed of the Lord, and that Charles was the usurper, he should have suffered any punishment rather than falsify his sentiments. It may be charitably supposed, however, that the events of the Restoration changed his opinion, and made him satisfied to be still a royalist. We have no evidence in any part of his life, that Mr. Eliot was a time-server, or coward; on the contrary, he was remarkable for decision of character and independence.

In confirmation of what has now been said respecting Mr. Eliot's decision and firmness, we may allude to the part he took in opposing the sentiments and influence of that notorious disturber of the churches in his day, Mrs. Anne Hutchinson. She was of the sect of Antinomians, who abused the doctrines of free grace, maintaining that the law is of no use or obligation under the dispensation of the Gospel, while the doctrines they taught superseded the necessity of good works. Mrs. Hutchinson pretended to immediate impressions from heaven as the rule of conduct, saying that she knew God "spake to her, just as Abraham knew that it was the command of Heaven to sacrifice Isaac." The Governor, Vane, who was an enthusiast, countenanced this woman, and Rev. Mr. Cotton, who took Mr. Eliot's place in the church at Boston, when Mr. Eliot removed to Roxbury, was also infected by her influence so far as to oppose his colleague, the Rev. Mr. Wilson, and the other ministers, who were generally opposed to her. Had Mr. Eliot remained the teacher of the church in Boston, it would have prevented that church from being divided as it was with regard to Mrs. Hutchinson, through the influence of his successor, Mr. Cotton. Mr. Eliot, with several other ministers, visited her, conversed with her upon religious subjects to ascertain her sentiments and spirit, and remonstrated with her for her bold denunciation of all the Plantation except Messrs. Cotton and Wheelright. Mr. Eliot appeared as a witness against her on her trial before the magistrates, and with Hugh Peters and Mr. Weld, testified that she said to them that "Mr. Cotton preached a covenant of grace, and the other ministers a covenant of works." Mr. Eliot added, "I do remember this also, that she said we were not able and faithful ministers of the new covenant, because we were not like the apostles before the ascension." Mr. Eliot took occasion on this trial to bear testimony against yielding to *impressions* as a rule of faith and duty. A passage from Mr. Hooker's sermons was quoted in justification of Mrs. Hutchinson's statements. But Mr. Eliot who had been brought up at the feet of Mr. Hooker, and knew his opinions well, insisted that the construction given to the passage was contrary to Mr. Hooker's mind and judgment. His old friend, Gov. Winthrop, gently dissented from Mr. Eliot's strong testimony against impressions. Mr. Eliot said, "I say there is an expectation of things promised; but to have a particular revelation of things, as they shall fall out, there is no such thing in the Scripture." Gov. Winthrop replied, "We must not limit the word of God." * Mrs. Hutchinson was condemned and banished. Her end softened the feelings of those who condemned her, and made them reflect upon the inexpediency of proceeding so strenuously as they did against her. Such feelings always arise in the minds of good men who have withstood prevailing errors, not to make them regret the testimony they bore for the truth, but to mourn over hasty and excessive zeal, when patience, and perhaps a measure of neglect, might sooner have ended a controversy, or have prevented it altogether. But it is easier for those who are removed, by time or place, from the excitements of a controversy, to moralize upon the best way of conducting it, than it would have been for them to exercise the judicious temper which they recommend and praise, had they themselves partaken in the strife. Mr. Eliot showed himself in this controversy to be no fanatical enthusiast, and gave

* Mass. Hist. Coll. 1802.

evidence that he was a man of decision and courage.

The following characteristic letter was written by the famous Rev. Richard Baxter to Dr. Increase Mather then in London. It was occasioned by the receipt of Cotton Mather's Life of Eliot.

"Dear Brother:

I thought I had been near dying at 12 o'clock, in bed; but your book revived me. I lay reading it until between one and two. I knew much of Mr. Eliot's opinions, by many letters which I had from him. There was no man on earth whom I honoured above him. It is his evangelical work that is the apostolical succession that I plead for. I am now dying, I hope, as he did. It pleased me to read from him my case, [*my understanding faileth, my memory faileth, my tongue faileth,*] (and my hand and pen,) *but my charity faileth not.* That word much comforted me. I am as zealous a lover of the New England Churches as any man, according to Mr. Noyes', Mr. Norton's, Mr. Mitchel's, and the Synod's model.

"I loved your father upon the letters I received from him. I love you better for your learning, labors, and peaceable moderation. I love your son better than either of you, for the excellent temper that appeareth in his writings.* O that godliness and wisdom (may) thus increase in all families! He hath honoured himself half as much as Mr. Eliot. I say but half as much; for deeds excel words. God preserve you and New England! Pray for

Your fainting,
languishing Friend,
RI. BAXTER."

August 3, 1691.

In contrast with the instructions which Mr. Eliot and other Protestant missionaries to the Indians gave the children of the wilderness, Cotton Mather alludes to the instructions given to the Indians in some parts of the country by the Popish missionaries. He says,

"By an odd accident there are lately fallen into my hands the manuscripts of a Jesuit, whom the French employed as a missionary among the western Indians, in which papers there are both a catechism, containing the principles which those heathens are to be instructed

* This testimony from Richard Baxter, in favor of the Mathers, is valuable to those who have seen them decried by some modern writers.

in, and cases of conscience referring to their conversations. The catechism, which is in the Iroquois language—with a translation annexed, has one chapter about heaven, and another about hell, wherein are such thick skulled passages as these."

Q. How is the soil made in heaven?

A. 'Tis a very fair soil, they want neither for meats nor clothes; 'tis but wishing, and we have them.

Q. Are they employed in heaven?

A. No, they do nothing; the fields yield corn, beans, pumpkins, and the like without any tillage.

Q. What sort of trees are there?

A. Always green, full, flourishing.

Q. Have they in heaven the same sun, the same wind, the same thunder that we have here?

A. No, the sun ever shines; it is always fair weather.

Q. But how are their fruits?

A. In this one quality they exceed ours, that they are never wasted; you have no sooner plucked one, but you see another presently hanging in its room.

Concerning hell, it thus discourses.

Q. What sort of a soil is that of hell?

A. A very wretched soil; 'tis a fiery pit in the centre of the earth.

Q. Have they any light in hell?

A. No. 'Tis always dark; there is always smoke there; their eyes are always in pain with it; they can see nothing but the devils.

Q. What shaped things are the devils?

A. Very ill shaped things; they go about with vizards on, and they terrify men.

Q. What do they eat in hell?

A. They are always hungry, but the damned feed on hot ashes and serpents there.

Q. What water do they drink?

A. Horrid water, nothing but melted lead.

Q. Don't they die in hell?

A. No; yet they eat one another every day; but anon, God restores and renews the man that was eaten, as a cropt plant in a little time repullulates.

One case of conscience is thus resolved by the Jesuit:

Q. Whether an Indian stealing a hatchet from a Dutchman be bound to make restitution?

A. If the Dutchman be one that has used any trade with other Indians, the thief is not bound unto any restitution; for it is certain he gains more by such a trade than the value of many hatchets in a year.

In the History of the Early Jesuit Missions to

the Indians of this country,* as well as in all other Jesuit missions, there is a degree of zeal and devotedness which is truly wonderful. This is not the place to discuss the motives of these men, nor the principle in human nature which leads to their self-sacrifice in the missionary work. The fruits of their work, however, show that they do not promulgate the Gospel of Christ in its simplicity, did we not know this by more direct evidence.

The wife of Mr. Eliot died three years before him, at the age of 84. She had come to him across the ocean, a betrothed bride, when he had found a home for her in this new world. During her residence here, "she had attained unto a considerable skill in physick and chirurgery which enabled her to dispense many safe, good, and useful medicines unto the poor that had occasion for them; and some hundreds of sick and weak and maimed people owed praises to God for the benefit which therein they freely received of her." †

She managed all the private affairs of her husband for him that he might devote his whole time and strength to his arduous public labors. She brought up his six children of whom he

* See Early Jesuit Missions, &c., by Wm. Ingraham Kip.

† C. Mather.

beautifully said, "they are all in Christ, or with Christ," and then she smoothed his passage to the tomb by going before him, and making him more willing to depart. "That one wife," says Mather, "which was given to him truly from the Lord, he loved, prized, cherished, with a kindness that notably represented the compassion which he thereby taught his church to expect from the Lord Jesus Christ; and after he had lived with her for more than half an hundred years he followed her to the grave with lamentations beyond those which the Jews, from the figure of a letter in the text,* affirm, that Abraham deplored his Sarah with; her departure made a deeper impression on him than what any common affliction could. His whole conversation with her had that sweetness and that gravity and modesty beautifying of it, that every one called them Zachery and Elizabeth." †

The old gray haired apostle stood over her coffin, and said to the concourse of people who had come to the funeral, "Here lies my dear, faithful, pious, prudent, prayerful wife. I

---

* Mather's allusion is probably this: In Gen. 23 : 2, where it is said that Abraham came to weep for Sarah, a letter, smaller than the rest, in the Hebrew word *to weep for her* is believed by the Jewish critics to intimate that his grief was somewhat composed; (—" luctum Abrahœ fuisse moderatum."—Poole's Synopsis.)—Ed.

† Magnalia I. 495.

shall go to her, but she shall not return to me."

Lord Bacon* speaking of "marriage and single life," tells us what wives are to young men, and that "for middle age" they are "companions," and "old men's nurses." Men generally do not wait till old age before they experience the exquisite tenderness and assiduity of woman in their sickness. We all subscribe to the last couplet of the following quotation, but not to the first:

> "O woman! in thine hours of ease
> Deceitful, coy. and hard to please.
> * * * * * *
> When pain and sickness wring the brow,
> A ministering angel thou."

There is a beautiful passage in one of Steele's papers in the Spectator. It purports to be a letter to his wife. He says.

"It is impossible for me to look back on many evils and pains which I have suffered since we came together, without a pleasure which is not to be expressed from the proofs I have had, in those circumstances, of your unmeasured goodness. How often has your tenderness removed pain from my sick head! how often anguish from my afflicted heart! With how skillful patience have I known you comply with the

---

* Essays, VIII.

vain projects which pain has suggested, to have an aching limb removed, by journeying from one side of a room to another! how often, the next instant, traveled the same ground again, *without telling your patient it was to no purpose to change his situation.* If there are such beings as guardian angels, thus are they employed. I will no more believe one of them more good in its inclinations, than I can conceive it more charming in its form than my wife."

As Mr. Eliot became disabled by age for the ministerial work, he seemed to have the earnest solicitude about a successor which Moses had when, towards the close of his life, he "cried to the Lord" that he would "set a man over the congregation." Mr. Eliot more than once assembled the people of the town to fast and pray with reference to a successor. The Rev. Nehemiah Walter was by the unanimous vote of the people associated with him in the pastoral office, after which it was with difficulty that he could be persuaded to conduct any public religious service, saying, "It would be a wrong to the souls of the people for him to do any thing among them when they were supplied so much to their advantage." The last time that he preached is said to have been on the occasion of a public fast, when he expounded the lxxxiii.

Psalm, being, (as the caption has it,) a complaint to God of the enemies' conspiracies, and a prayer against them that oppress the church. He concluded his exposition with an apology, begging his hearers to pardon the poorness and meanness and brokenness of his meditations, adding, " my dear brother here will by and by mend all."

He once expressed the fear that his old friends and neighbors, Messrs. Cotton, of Boston, and Mather, of Dorchester, who had gone to heaven before him, would suspect him to have gone the wrong way, because he staid so long behind them.

Towards the close of his life his mind dwelt much on the coming of the Son of Man, and whatever theme he began to converse upon, he soon fell into a strain of remarks upon this subject. On one occasion some one brought him intelligence of certain sad events whereby the Churches of New England were much afflicted. His reply was, " Behold some of the clouds in which we must look for the coming of the Son of Man."

Mr. Walter coming in to see him on his dying bed, Mr. Eliot said, " Brother, thou art welcome to my very soul. Pray retire to thy study for me, and give me leave to be gone," meaning that he should pray for his speedy release.

Being asked how he did, he said, " Alas, I have lost every thing; my understanding leaves me, my memory fails me; my utterance fails me; but I thank God my charity holds out still; I find that rather grows than fails."

Speaking of the work in which he had been engaged among the Indians, he said, " There is a cloud, a dark cloud, upon the work of the gospel, among the poor Indians. The Lord revive and prosper that work, and grant that it may live when I am dead. It is a work which I have been doing much and long about. But what was the word I spoke last? I recall that word, *my doings!* Alas! they have been poor and small, and lean doings; and I'll be the man that shall throw the first stone at them all."

The Rev. Increase Mather had gone to England on business connected with the ecclesiastical affairs of New England. Mr. Eliot wrote the following letter to him, and it is the last writing of his of which we have any account.

" Reverend and beloved Mr. Increase Mather.

I cannot write. Read Neh. 2: 10. When Sanballat the Horonite, and Tobiah the servant, the Ammonite heard of it, it grieved them exceedingly that there was come a man to seek the welfare of the children of Israel.

"Let thy blessed soul feed full and fat upon this and other Scriptures. All other things I leave to other men, and rest,

Your loving Brother,

JOHN ELIOT."

One of Mr. Eliot's last expressions was this, Welcome joy! His last breath was spent in calling upon those who stood around his dying bed to "Pray, Pray, Pray." He died in the beginning of the year 1690, in the eighty-sixth year of his age.

Before his death, Mr. Eliot had the pleasure of seeing several faithful men raised up to labor among the Indians; among whom were Daniel Gookin, James Noyce, Rowland Cotton, Peter Thacher, Grindal Rawson, Goddefred Dettins, and M. Bondet. Mather says, "about the year 1700, through the blessing of God in this one Massachusetts province, the Indians have mostly embraced the Christian religion. There are I suppose, more than thirty congregations of Indians, and many more than three thousand Indians, in this one province, calling on God in Christ, and hearing of his glorious Word."

In writing these pages, I have before me a copy of Eliot's Indian Bible, to which are annexed his Psalms and Hymns, in the Indian tongue, and a short Catechism. Here is the monument of John Eliot; and what monument of earthly greatness is to be compared with it! The kings of the earth sleep in the great cathedral; the beautiful, ivy grown, ruined abbey crowns the sepulchre of the novelist and poet; the marble statue immortalizes the name and deeds of the conqueror by land or sea. They are but the grass that withereth, and the flower which fadeth, "but the word of the Lord endureth forever." "Endureth"? There is not one Indian on this continent, or on the face of the earth, that can read this book. It can never guide another soul to God. As you look upon its title page, written in an unknown tongue, you see these words, Up-Biblum God, the Book of God. How significant, we may say, the appearance of those words when we consider the condition of the book bereaved of the race who once read it. "Up-Biblum God." Like the man-child of the woman clothed with the sun who fled into the wilderness, and whose child was caught up unto God, and to his throne, this book, having done its office here, is, in a certain sense, caught up to God; and there it "endureth forever," in the hearts and souls of redeemed savages.

This book will never, of course, be reprinted, and copies of it are becoming rare. But if we wished to send something to a desponding missionary, or an example of condescension and love for souls to a minister who despises and neglects his poor, humble people, no better gift could be selected than a copy of Eliot's Bible. What gentle rebuke, what exhortation and encouragement, its long barbarous words would speak oftentimes in the minister's or missionary's study. We might appropriately inscribe on its cover the third reflection of Mr. Eliot on returning from one of his visits to Nonantum, and send it to every missionary station round the globe: "There is no need of miraculous or extraordinary gifts in seeking the salvation of the most depraved of the human family."

The mention of this Bible may lead us to think of that half million of wild Indians and that million and a half of partly civilized Indians who now occupy the wilderness of the west. It bids us attempt their conversion; it shows us that no difficulties are too mighty for the Gospel to overcome, no discouragements too great for true Christian faith and courage. The objects of our forefathers' zeal and hope in coming to these shores, are now beyond the Rocky Mountains. A wilderness still invites our increasing missionary efforts, as a wilderness once invited the labors of the Pilgrims. Wronged and driven away by the white man, still they cry :

APPENDIX.

A.—See page 201.

(Coll. Mass. Hist. Soc. 1732.)

"The following fabulous Traditions and Customs of the Indians of Martha's Vineyard, were communicated to Benjamin Basset, Esq. of Chilmark, by Thomas Cooper, a half blooded Indian, of Gay head, aged about sixty years; and which, he says, he obtained of his grandmother, who, to use his own expression, was a stout girl, when the English came to the island.

The first Indian who came to the Vineyard, was brought thither with his dog on a cake of ice. When he came to Gay Head, he found a very large man, whose name was Moshup. He had a wife and five children, four sons and one daughter; and lived in the Den. He used to catch whales, and then pluck up trees, and make a fire, and roast them. The coals of the trees, and the bones of the whales, are now to be seen.

After he was tired of staying here, he told his children to go and play ball on a beach that joined Noman's Land to Gay Head. He then made a mark with his toe across the beach at each end, and so deep, that the water followed, and cut away the beach; so that his children were in fear of drowning. They took their sister up, and held her out of the water. He told them to act as if they were going to kill whales; and they were all turned into killers, (a fish so called.) The sister was dressed in large stripes. He gave them a strict charge always to be kind to her. His wife mourned the loss of her children so exceedingly, that he threw her away. She fell upon Seconet, near the rocks, where she lived some time, exacting contribution of all who passed by water. After a while she was changed into a stone. The entire shape remained for many years. But after the English came, some of them broke off the arms, head, &c. but the most of the body remains to this day. Moshup went away nobody knows whither. He had no conversation with the Indians, but was kind to them, by sending whales, &c. ashore to them to eat. But after they grew thick around him he left them.

Whenever the Indians worshipped, they always sang and danced, and then begged of the sun and moon, as they thought most likely to hear them, to send them the desired favour; most generally rain or fair weather, or freedom from their enemies or sickness.

Before the English came among the Indians, there were two disorders of which they most generally died, viz. the consumption and the yellow fever. The latter they could always *lay* in the following manner. After it had raged and swept off a number, those who were well met to lay it. The rich, that is, such as had a canoe, skins, axes, &c. brought them. They took their seat in a circle; and all the poor sat around, without. The richest then proposed to begin to lay the sickness; and having in his hand something in shape resembling his canoe, skin, or whatever his riches were, he threw it up in the air; and whoever of the poor without could take it, the property it was intended to resemble became forever transferred to him or her. After the rich had thus given away all their moveable property to the poor, they looked out the handsomest and most sprightly young man in the assembly, and put him into an entire new wigwam, built of every thing new for that purpose. They then formed into two files at a small distance from each other. One standing in the space at each end, put fire to the bottom

24*

of the wigwam on all parts, and fell to singing and dancing. Presently the youth would leap out of the flames, and fall down to appearance dead. Him they committed to the care of five virgins, prepared for that purpose, to restore to life again. The term required for this would be uncertain, from six to forty-eight hours; during which time the dance must be kept up. When he was restored, he would tell, that he had been carried in a large thing high up in the air, where he came to a great company of white people, with whom he had interceded hard to have the distemper layed; and generally after much persuasion, would obtain a promise, or answer of peace which never failed of laying the distemper."

"*Inscription copied from a grave stone at Gay Head.*

1 2 3
YEUUH'WOHHOK'SIPSIN'

4 5
SIL'PAUL'NOHTOBEYONTOK'

6 7
AGED' 49: YEARS'NUPPOOP'TAH'

AUGUST'24TH1787.

EXPLANATIONS.

1. *Here.* 2. *The body.* 3. *Lies.* 4. *Silas Paul.* 5. *An ordained preacher.* 6. *Died.* 7. *Then,* or *in.*"

B.—See page 41.

In connection with the remarks in the foregoing pages on the climate and soil of New England, the following extract from a piece by Rev. John Higginson of Salem, 1629, will be read with interest. It is taken from the Collections of the Mass. Hist. Society, 1792.

NEW-ENGLANDS PLANTATION.

Or, a short and true DESCRIPTION of the Commodities and Discommodities of that countrey. Written in the year 1629, by Mr. HIGGESON, a Reverend Divine, now there resident. Whereunto is added a Letter, sent by Mr. GRAVES, an Enginere, out of New-England. Reprinted from the third edition, London, 1530.

LETTING passe our voyage by sea,* we will now begin our discourse on the shore of New-England. And because the life and wel-fare of every creature heere below, and the commodiousnesse of the countrey whereat such creatures live, doth by the most wise ordering of God's

* For the Journal of Mr. Higginson's Voyage, see Hutchinson's Collection of Papers, page 32.

providence, depend next unto himselfe, upon the temperature and disposition of the foure elements, earth, water, aire, and fire (for as of the mixture of all these, all sublunary things are composed; so by the more or lesse enjoyment of the wholesome temper and convenient use of these, consisteth the onely well-being both of man and beast in a more or lesse comfortable measure in all countreys under the heavens) therefore I will indeavour to shew you what New-England is by the consideration of each of these apart, and truly indeavour by God's helpe to report nothing but the naked truth, and that both to tell you of the discommodities as well as of the commodities, though as the idle proverbe is, *travellers may lye by authoritie*, and so may take too much sinfull libertie that way. Yet I may say of my selfe as once Nehemiah did in another case: *Shall such a man as I lye?* No verily: It becommeth not a preacher of truth to be a writer of falshod in any degree: And therefore I have beene carefull to report nothing of New-England but what I have partly seene with mine own eyes, and partly heard and enquired from the mouths of verie honest and religious persons, who, by living in the countrey a good space of time, have had experience and knowledge of the state thereof, and whose testimonies I doe beleeve as my selfe.

First therefore of the earth of New-England and all the appertenances thereof: It is a land of divers and sundry sorts all about Masathulets Bay, and at Charles river is as fat blacke earth as can be seene any where: and in other places you have a clay soyle, in other gravell, in other sandy, as it is all about our plantation at Salem, for so our towne is now named. Psal. 76: 2.

The forme of the earth here in the superfices of it is neither too flat in the plainnesse, nor too high in hils, but partakes of both in a mediocritie, and fit for pasture, or for plow or meddow ground, as men please to employ it: though all the countrey bee as it were a thicke wood for the generall, yet in divers places there is much ground cleared by the Indians, and especially about the plantation: And I am told that about three miles from us a man may stand on a little hilly place and see divers thousands of acres of ground as good as need to be, and not a tree in the same. It is thought here is good clay to make bricke and tyles and earthen-pot as need to be. At this instant we are setting a brick-kill on worke to make brickes and tiles for the building of our houses. For stone, here is plentie of slates at the Isle of Slate in Masathulets bay, and lime-stone, free-stone, and smooth-stone, and iron-stone, and marble-stone also in such store, that we have great rocks of it, and a harbour hard by. Our plantation is from thence called Marble-harbour.

Of minerals there hath yet beene but little triall made, yet we are not without great hope of being furnished in that soyle.

The fertilitie of the soyle is to be admired at, as appeareth in the aboundance of grasse that groweth everie where, both verie thicke, verie long, and verie high in divers places: But it groweth verie wildly with a great stalke and a broad and ranker blade, because it never had been eaten with cattle, nor mowed with a sythe, and seldome trampled on by foot. It is scarce to bee beleeved how our kine and goates, horses and hogges, doe thrive and prosper here and like well of this countrey.

In our plantation we have already a quart of milke for a penny: but the aboundant encrease of corne proves this countrey to bee a wonderment. Thirtie, fortie, fiftie, sixtie are ordinarie here: Yea Joseph's encrease in Ægypt is outstript here with us. Our planters hope to have more then a hundred fould this yere: And all this while I am within compasse; what will you say of two hundred fould and upwards? It is almost incredible what great gaine some of our English planters have had by our Indiane corne. Credible persons have assured me, and the partie himselfe avouched the truth of it to me, that of the setting of 13 gallons of corne hee hath had encrease of it 52 hogsheads, every hogshead holding seven bushels of London measure, and every bushell was by him sold and trusted to the Indians for so much beaver as was worth 13 shillings; and so of this 13 gallons of corne, which was worth 6 shillings 8 pence, he made about 327 pounds of it the yeere following, as by reckoning will appeare: where you may see how God blessed husbandry in this land. There is not such greate and plentifull eares of corne I suppose any where else to bee found but in this countrey: Because also of varietie of colours, as red, blew, and yellow, &c. and of one corne there springeth four or five hundred. I have sent you many eares of divers colours that you might see the truth of it.

Little children here by setting of corne may earne much more then their owne maintenance.

They have tryed our English corne at New Plimmouth plantation, so that all our several graines will grow here verie well, and have a fitting soyle for their nature.

Our Governor hath store of greene pease growing in his garden, as good as ever I eat in England.

This country aboundeth naturally with store of roots of great varitie and good to eat. Our turnips, parsnips, and carrots are here both bigger and sweeter then is ordinary to be found in England. Here are store of pumpions, cowcombers, and other things of that nature which I know not. Also divers excellent pot-herbs grow abundantly among the grasse, as strawberrie leaves in all places of the countrey, and plentie of strawberries in their time, and pennyroyall, wintersaverie, sorrell, brookelime, liverwort, carvell, and watercresses, also leekes and onions are ordinarie, and divers physicall herbs. Here are also aboundance of other sweet herbs delightful to the smell, whose names we know not, &c. and plentie of single damaske roses verie sweete; and two kinds of herbes that bare two kinds of flowers very sweet, which they say, are as good to make cordage or cloath as any hempe or flaxe we have.

Excellent vines are here up and downe in the woods. Our Governour hath already planted a vineyard with great hope of encrease.

Also, mulberries, plums, raspberries, corrance, chesnuts, filberds, walnuts, smalnuts, hurtleberies, and hawes of whitethorne neere as good as our cherries in England, they grow in plentie here.

For wood there is no better in the world I thinke, here being foure sorts of oke differing both in the leafe, timber, and colour, all excellent good. There is also good ash, elme, willow, birch, beech, saxafras, juniper, cipres, cedar, spruce, pines, and firre that will yeeld abundance of turpentine, pitch, tarre, masts, and other materials for building both of ships and houses. Also here are store of sumacke trees, they are good for dying and tanning of leather, likewise such trees yeeld a precious gem called wine benjamin, that they say is excellent for perfumes. Also here be divers roots and berries wherewith the Indians dye excellent holding colours that no raine nor washing can alter. Also, wee have materials to make sope-ashes and salt-peter in aboundance.

For beasts there are some beares, and they say some *lyons* also; for they have been seen at Cape Anne. Also here are several sorts of deere, some whereof bring three or four young ones at once, which is not ordinarie in England. Also wolves, foxes, beavers, otters, martins, great wild cats, and a great beast called a molke as bigge as an oxe. I have seen the skins of all these beasts since I came to this plantation excepting lyons. Also here are great store of squerrels, some greater, and some smaller and lesser: there are some of the lesser sort, they tell me, that by a certaine skill will fly from tree to tree, though they stand farre distant.

Of the waters of New-England, *with the things belonging to the same.*

New-England hath water enough, both salt and fresh, the greatest sea in the world, the Atlanticke sea, runs all along the coast thereof. There are abundance of Ilands along the shore, some full of wood and masts to feed swine; and others cleere of wood, and fruitful to bear corne. Also wee have store of excellent harbours for ships, as at Cape Anne, and at Masathulets Bay, and at Salem, and at many other places: and they are the better because for strangers there is a verie difficult and dangerous passage into them, but unto such as are well acquainted with them, they are easie and safe enough. The aboundance of sea-fish are almost beyond beleeving, and sure I should scarce have beleeved it, except I had seene it with mine owne eyes.

I saw great store of whales, and crampusse, and such aboundance of mackerils that it would astonish one to behold, likewise cod-fish in aboundance on the coast, and in their season are plentifully taken. There is a fish called a basse, a most sweet and wholesome fish as ever I did eate, it is altogether as good as our fresh sammon, and the season of their comming was begun when wee came first to New-England in June, and so continued about three months space. Of this fish our fishers take many hundreds together, which I have seen lying on the shore to my admiration; yea their nets ordinarily take more than they are able to hale to land, and for want of boats and men they are constrained to let a many goe after they have taken them, and yet sometimes they fill two boates at a time with them. And besides basse wee take plentie of scate and thornbacks, and abundance of lobsters and the least boy in the plantation may both catch and eat what he will of them. For my owne part I was soone cloyed with them, they were so great, and fat, and lussious. I have seene some myselfe that have weighed 16 pound, but others have had divers times so great lobsters as have weighed 25 pound, as they assure mee. Also heere is abundance of herring, turbut, sturgion, cuskes, hadocks, mullets, eeles, crabbes, muskles, and oysters. Besides there is probability that the countrey is of an excellent temper for the making of salt: For since our comming our fishermen have brought home very good salt which they found candied by the standing of the sea water and the heat of the sunne, upon a rocke by the sea shore: and in divers salt marishes that some have gone through, they have found some salt in some places crushing under their feete and cleaving to their shooes.

And as for fresh water, the countrey is full of dainty springs, and some great rivers, and some lesser brookes; and at Masathulets Bay they digged wels and found water at three foot deepe in most places: And neere Salem thay have as fine cleare water as we can desire, and we may digge wels and find water where we list.

Thus wee see both land and sea abound with store of blessings for the comfortable sustenance of man's life in New-England.

Of the aire of New-England *with the temper and creatures in it.*

The temper of the aire of New-England is one speciall thing that commends this place. Experience doth manifest that there is hardly a more healthfull place to be found in the world that agreeth better with our English bodyes. Many that have been weake and sickly in old England, by comming hither have beene thoroughly healed and growne healthfull strong. For here is an extraordinarie cleere and dry aire that is of a most healing nature to all such as are of a cold, melancholy, flegmatick, rheumatick temper of body. None can more truly speake hereof by their owne experience then my selfe. My friends that knew me can well tell how verie sickly I have bin and continually in physick, being much troubled with a tormenting paine through an extraordinarie weaknesse of my stomacke, and aboundance of melancholicke humors; but since I came hither on this voyage, I thanke God, I have had perfect health, and freed from paine and vomiting, having a stomacke to digest the hardest and coursest fare, who before could not eat finest meat; and whereas my stomache could onely digest and did require such drinke as was both strong and stale, now I can and doe often times drink New-England water verie well; and I that have not gone without a cap for many yeeres together, neither durst leave off the same, have now cast away my cap, and doe weare none at all in the day time: And whereas beforetime I cloathed my selfe with double cloaths and thicke waistcoates to keep me warme, even in the summer time, I doe now goe as thin clad as any, onely wearing a light stuffe cassocke upon my shirt, and stuffe breeches of one thickness without linings. Besides I have one of my children that was formerly most lamentably handled with sore breaking out of both his hands and feet of the king's-evill, but since he came hither hee is very well ever he was, and there is hope of perfect recoverie shortly even by the very wholesomnesse of the aire, altering, digesting and drying up the cold and crude humours of the body: And therefore I thinke it is a wise course for al cold complections to come to take physick in New-England: for a sup of New-England's aire is better then a whole draught of Old England's ale.

In the summer time, in the midst of July and August, it is a good deale hotter then in Old England: And in winter, January and February are much colder, as they say: But the spring and autumne are of a middle temper.

Fowles of the aire are plentifull here, and of all sorts as we have in England, as farre as I can learn, and a great many of strange fowles which we know not. Whilst I was writing these things, one of our men brought home an eagle which hee had killed in the wood: They say they are good meate. Also here are many kinds of excellent hawkes, both sea hawkes and land hawkes: And my self walking in the woods with another in company, sprung a patridge so bigge that through the heaviness of his body could fly but a little way: They that have killed them, say they are as bigge as our hens. Here are likewise aboundance of turkies often killed in the woods, farre greater then our English turkies, and exceeding fat, sweet, and fleshy, for here they have aboundance of feeding all the yeere long, as strawberries, in summer al places are full of them, and all manner of berries and fruits. In the winter time I have seene flockes of pidgeons, and have eaten of them: They doe fly from tree to tree as other birds doe, which our pidgeons will not doe in England: They are of all colours as ours are, but their wings and tayles are far longer, and therefore it is likely they fly swifter to escape the terrible hawkes in this country. In winter time this country doth abound with wild geese, wild ducks, and other sea fowle, that a great part of winter the planters have eaten nothing but roast-meate of divers fowles which they have killed.

Thus you have heard of the earth, water and aire of New-England, now it may bee you expect something to bee said of the fire proportionable to the rest of the elements. Indeede I thinke New-England may boast of this element more then of all the rest: For though it bee here somewhat cold in the winter, yet here we have plenty of fire to warme us, and that a great deal cheaper then they sel billets and faggots in London: Nay, all Europe is not able to afford to make so great fires as New-England. A poore servant here that is to possesse but 50 acres of land, may afford to give more wood for timber and fire as good as the world yeelds, then many noble men in England can afford to do. Here is good living for those that love good fires. And although New-England have no tallow to make candles of, yet by the aboundance of the fish thereof, it can afford oil for lampes. Yea our pine-trees that are the most plentifull of all wood, doth allow us plenty of candles which are very usefull in a house: And they are such candles as the Indians commonly use, having no other, and they are nothing else but the wood of the pine tree cloven in two little slices, something thin, which are so full of the moysture of turpentine and pitch, that they burne as cleere as a torch. I have sent you some of them that you may see the experience of them.

Thus of New-England's commodities: now I will tell you of some discommodities that are here to be found.

First, in the summer season for these three months, June, July, and August, we are troubled much with little flyes called musketoes, being the same they are troubled with in Lincolneshire and the Fens; and they are nothing but gnats, which except they bee smoked out of their houses are troublesome in the night season.

Secondly, in the winter season for two months space, the earth is commonly covered with snow, which is accompanied with sharp biting frosts, something more sharpe then is in Old England, and therefore are forced to make great fires.

Thirdly, the countrey being very full of woods, and wildernesses, doth also much abound with snakes and serpents of strange colours, and huge greatnesse: yea there are some serpents called rattle-snakes that have rattles in their tailes, that will not fly from a man as others will, but will flye upon him, and sting him so mortally, that hee will dye within a quarter of an houre after, except the partie stinged have about him some of the root of an herbe called snake-weed to bite on, and then hee shall receive no harme: but yet seldom falles it out that any hurt is done by these. About three years since, an Indian was stung to death by one of them, but wee heard of none since that time.

Fourthly and lastly, here wants as it were

good company of honest christians to bring with them horses, kine, and sheepe, to make use of this fruitfull land: great pitty it is to see so much good ground for corne and for grasse as any is under the heavens, to ly altogether unoccupied, when so many honest men and their families in Old England through the populousnesse thereof, do make evry hard shift to live one by the other.

Now, thus you know what New-England is, as also with the commodities and discommodities thereof: Now I will shew you a little of the inhabitants thereof, and their government.

For their governors they have kings, which they call Saggamores, some greater, and some lesser, according to the number of their subjects.

The greatest Saggamores about us can not make above three hundred men,* and other lesse Saggamores have not above fifteen subjects, and others neere about us but two.

Their subjects above twelve years since † were swept away by a great and grievous plague that was amongst them, so that there are verie few left to inhabite the country.

The Indians are not able to make use of the one fourth part of the land, neither have they any settled places, as townes to dwell in, nor

* That is fighting men.

† 1617.

any ground as they challenge for their own possession, but change their habitation from place to place.

For their statures, they are a tall and strong limmed people, their colours are tawney, they goe naked, save onely they are in part covered with beasts skins on one of their shoulders, and weare something before; their haire is generally blacke, and cut before like our gentlewomen, and one locke longer than the rest, much like to our gentelmen, which fashion I thinke came from hence into England.

For their weapons, they have bowes and arrowes, some of them headed with bone, and some with brasse: I have sent you some of them for an example.

The men for the most part live idely, they do nothing but hunt and fish: Their wives set their corne and doe all their other worke. They have little houshold stuffe, as a kettle, and some other vessels like trayes, spoones, dishes, and baskets.

Their houses are verie little and homely, being made with small poles pricked into the ground, and so bended and fastened at the tops, and on the sides they are matted with boughs and covered on the roof with sedge and old mats, and for their beds that they take their rest on, they have a mat.

They doe generally professe to like well of our coming and planting here; partly because their is abundance of ground that they cannot possesse nor make use of, and partly because our being here will bee a meanes both of relief to them when they want, and also a defence from their enemies, wherewith (I say) before this plantation began, they were often indangered.

For their religion they do worship two Gods, a good God and an evil God: The good God they call Tantum, and their evil God whom they fear will doe them hurt, they call Squantum.

For their dealing with us, we neither fear them nor trust them, for fourtie of our musketeeres will drive five hundred of them out of the field. We use them kindly; they will come into our houses sometimes by half a dozen or half a score at a time when we are at victuals, but will ask or take nothing but what we give them.

We purpose to learn their language as soon as we can, which will be a means to do them good.

Of the present condition of the Plantation, and what it is.

WHEN we came first to Nehum-kek,* we found about half a score houses, and a faire house

* Or Naumkeag. Salem.

newly built for the Governor, we found also aboundance of corne planted by them, very good and well liking. And we brought with us about two hundred passengers and planters more, which by common consent of the old planters were all combined together into one body politicke, under the same Governour.

There are in all of us both old and new planters about three hundred, whereof two hundred of them are settled at Nehum-kek, now called Salem: And the rest have planted themselves at Masathulets Bay, beginning to build a towne there which wee do call Cherton, or Charles Town.

We that are settled at Salem make what haste we can to build houses, so that within a short time we shall have a faire towne.

We have great ordnance, wherewith we doubt not but we shall fortifie ourselves in a short time to keepe out a potent adversary. But that which is our greatest comfort, and meanes of defence above all other, is, that we have here the true religion and holy ordinances of Almighty God taught amongst us: Thankes be to God, wee have here plenty of preaching, and diligent catechizing, with strict and carefull exercise, and good and commendable orders to bring our people into a christian conversation with whom we have to doe withall. And thus wee doubt not but God will be with us, and *if God be with us, who can be against us?*

[Here ends Master Higgeson's relation of New-England.]

A letter sent from New England, by Master GRAVES, *Engynere, now there resident.*

THUS much I can affirme in generall, that I never came in a more goodly country in all my life, all things considered: If it hath not at any time been manured and husbanded, yet it is very beautifull in open lands, mixed with goodly woods, and again open plaines, in some places five hundred acres, some places more, some lesse, not much troublesome for to cleer for the plough to goe in, no place barren, but on the tops of the hils; the grasse and weeds grow up to a man's face, in the lowlands and by fresh rivers, aboundance of grasse and large meddowes without any tree or shrubbe to hinder the sith. I never saw, except in Hungaria, unto which I alwayes paralell this countrie, in all our most respects, for every thing that is heare eyther sowne or planted prospereth far better then in Old-England: The increase of corne is here farre beyond expectation, as I have seene here by experience in barly, the which because it is so much above your conception I will not mention. And cattle doe prosper very well, and those that are bredd here farr greater than those with you in England. Vines doe grow here plentifully laden with the biggest grapes that ever I saw, some I have seen foure inches about, so that I am bold to say of this countrie, as it is commonly said in Germany of Hungaria, that for cattel, corne, and wine it excelleth. We have many more hopefull commodities here in this country, the which time will teach to make good use of: In the mean time wee abound with such things which next under God doe make us subsist: as fish, foule, deere, and sundrie sorts of fruits, as musk-millions, water-millions, Indian pompions, Indian pease, beanes, and many other odde fruits that I cannot name; all which are made good and pleasant through this maine blessing of God, the healthfulnesse of the countrie which far exceedeth all parts that ever I have beene in: It is observed that few or none doe here fal sicke, unless of the scurvy, that they bring from aboard the ship with them, whereof I have cured some of my companie onely by labour.

C.—See page 204.

See Morell's poem on New England, Mass. Hist. Coll., 1792.

D.—See page 222.

The following letter to King Charles II. accompanied the presentation of the New Testament in the Indian tongue. The letter was written and sent by the Commissioners of the United Colonies of Massachusetts, Plymouth, Connecticut and New Haven.

"To the High and Mighty Prince, Charles the second, by the grace of God, King of England, Scotland, France, and Ireland, Defender of the faith, &c.

"The Commissioners of the United Colonies in New England, wish increase of all happiness.

"Most dread Sovereign,

"If our weak apprehensions have not misled us, this work will be no unacceptable present to your Majesty, as having a greater interest therein, than we believe is generally understood, which upon this occasion we conceive it our duty to declare.

"The people of these four colonies (confederate for mutual defence, in the times of the late distractions of our dear native country) your Majesty's natural born subjects, by the favour and grace of your royal father and grandfather of famous memory, put themselves upon this great and hazardous undertaking, of planting themselves at their own charge in these remote ends of the earth; that without offence or provocation to our dear brethren and countrymen, we might enjoy that liberty to worship God, which our own conscience informed us was not only our right but duty; as also that we, if it so pleased God, might be instrumental to spread the light of the gospel, the knowledge of the son of God, our saviour, to the poor, barbarous heathen; which by his late Majesty, in some of our patents, is declared to be the principal aim.

"These honest and pious intentions have through the grace of God and our kings, been seconded with proportionable success. For, omitting the immunities indulged by your Highness's royal predecessors, we have been greatly encouraged by your Majesty's gracious expressions of favour and approbation, signified unto the address made by the principal of our colonies; to which the rest do most cordially subscribe; though wanting the like seasonable opportunity, they have been till now deprived of the means to congratulate your Majesty's happy restitution, after your long sufferings; which we implore may yet be graciously accepted, that we may be equal partakers of your royal favour and moderation; which hath been so illustrious, that to admiration, the animosities of different persuasions of men have been so soon composed, and so much cause of hope, that, unless the sins of the nation prevent, a blessed calm will succeed the late horrid confusions of church and state. And shall not we, dread sovereign, your subjects of these colonies, of the same faith and belief in all points of doctrine with our countrymen and other reformed churches, though perhaps not alike persuaded in some matters of order, which in outward respects hath been unhappy for us,—promise and assure ourselves of all just favour and indulgence from a prince so graciously and happily endowed?

"The other part of our errand hither hath been attended with endeavours and blessing; many of the wild Indians being taught, and understanding, the doctrine of the christian religion, and with much affection attending such preachers as are sent to teach them. Many of their children are instructed to write and read; and some of them have proceeded further to attain the knowledge of the Latin and the Greek tongues, and are brought up with our English youth in university learning. There are divers of them that can and do read some parts of the scripture, and some catechisms which formerly have been translated into their own language: which hath occasioned the undertaking of a great work, viz. the printing the whole bible: which, being translated by a painful labourer among them, who was desirous to see the work accomplished in his days, hath already proceeded to the finishing of the new testament; which we here humbly present to your Majesty, as the first fruit and accomplishment of the pious design of your royal ancestors. The old testament is now under the press, wanting and craving your royal favour and assistance for the perfecting thereof.

"We may not conceal, though this work hath been begun and prosecuted by such instruments as God has raised up here; yet the chief charge and cost, which hath supported and carried it thus far, hath been from the charity and piety of divers of our well affected countrymen in England; who, being sensible of our inability in that respect, and studious to promote so good a work, contributed large sums of money, which were to be improved according to the direction and order of the then prevailing powers; which hath been faithfully and religiously attended, both there and here, according to the pious intentions of the benefactors. And we most humbly beseech your Majesty, that a matter of so much devotion and piety, tending so much to the honour of God, may suffer no disappointment through any legal defect, without the fault of the donors, or poor Indians, who only receive the benefit; but that your Majesty be graciously pleased to establish and confirm the same; being contrived and done, as we conceive, in that first year of your Majesty's reign, of this book was begun and now finished the first year of your establishment: which doth not only presage the happy success of your Highness's government, but will be a perpetual monument, that by your Majesty's favour, the gospel of our Lord Jesus Christ was made known to the Indians; an honour whereof, we are assured, your Majesty will not a little esteem.

"Sir, the shine of your royal favour upon these undertakings will make these tender plants to flourish, notwithstanding any malevolent aspect from those that bear evil will to this Sion; and render your Majesty more illustrious and glorious to after generations.

"The God of heaven long preserve and bless your Majesty with many happy days, to his glory, the good and comfort of his church and people. Amen."

E.—See page 182.

The Society for Propagating the Gospel among the Indians has been mentioned several times in this work.

About the year 1648, during the Protectorate of Cromwell, when the Presbyterians and Independents had influence in England, a Society was formed through the influence, it is believed, of Gov. Winslow, and called the Society for Propagating the Gospel among the Indians and others in North America.

It is somewhere stated respecting Cromwell that he had conceived a very extensive scheme for the universal propagation of the Gospel, borrowing the zeal and ingenuity of the Jesuits, and intending to meet and counteract their efforts everywhere. This scheme perished with him in his early death. Even the Society for Propagating the Gospel among the Indians, &c., did not long survive the restoration of royalty in 1660. But during its existence under the Commonwealth it rendered aid to Mayhew, Eliot, and others, the funds being applied here through the Commissioners of the four Colonies.

The Society being dissolved at the Restoration of monarchy under Charles II., an urgent application was soon made for another Society having the same name and objects. The honorable and distinguished Robert Boyle was President of the new Society. He had great wealth, and used it with profuse liberality. The celebrated Bishop Burnet was his almoner in many private as well as public charities. He distributed a thousand pounds a year for several years before his death among the French refugees in England. He also gave yearly, for a long time, the sum of three hundred pounds for the propagation of the Gospel in North America. Mr. Eliot's letters to his noble benefactor, which may be found in the Collections of the Mass. Hist. Society, will be read with interest.

The Indian School, at Cambridge, was supported by the funds of this Society, and a building erected for it by the same. In 1665 there were eight Indian youths in that school. Eliot's Indian Bible was printed at the expense of this Society, and cost £500, or not far from two thousand dollars.

For a few years, the General Court of Massachusetts granted five hundred dollars towards the object of this Society. At the suggestion of the Society the Governor issued a request for contributions in its behalf to the towns of the Commonwealth. About $1560 were collected.

This Society continues to this time. In 1800, its funds amounted to $20.000. At present they are not far from twice that sum. It is in the hands of members of the Unitarian denomination.*

F.

Letters of Mr. Eliot to Hon. Robert Boyle may be found in Mass. Hist. Coll. 1792. Also two interesting letters from the same in Frances' Life of Eliot, pp. 250 and 267.

G.

See, for an account of the Missionary Labors of the Mayhews, Wilson's Memoirs of Eliot, pp. 273—9.

H.

See Wilson's Memoirs of E., p. 290.

* See Smith & Choules' Hist. Miss. 1832, Vol. II.

I.

Mr. Eliot's Observations on forming the Indian Alphabet, do. do., p. 284.

K.

For an account of Rev. William Leverich, and some other laborers among the Indians, see Wilson's Memoirs, pp. 257–60. p. 278–99.

L.—See page 133.

The following petitions of Mr. Eliot have been copied for this work from the Mass. State Papers. The first is a temperance document which has not lost any pertinency or force by age.

Petition of John Eliot to the ——— General Court concerning the Indians,

SHEWETH,

That whereas the Indians have frequent recourse to English townes and especially to Boston where they too often see evil examples of excessive drinking with English who are too often disgraced with that beastly sin of drunkenness. And themselves many of them greatly delighting in strong liquors, not considering the strength and evil of them, and also too well knowing the liberty of the law which prohibiteth above half a pint of wine to a man that therefore they may without offence to the law have their half pint, and when they have had it in one place they goe to another and have the like till they be drunken. And sometime find too much entertainment that way by such who keepe no ordinary only desire theire trade though it be with the hurt and perdition of their soules. Therefore my humble request unto this honored Court is this, that there may be but one ordinary in all Boston who may have liberty to sell wine or any strong drink unto the Indians. And that whoever shall further them in their vicious drinking for theire own base ends who keep no ordinary may not be suffered in such a sinne without due punishment. And that at what ordinary soever in any other towne as well as Boston any Indian shall be found drunk, having had any considerable quantity of drink there, they should come under severe censure. These things I am bold to present unto you for the preventing of those scandalous evils which greatly blemish and interrupt their entertainment of the Gospel through the policy of Satan who counter worketh Christ with not a little uncomfortable success. And thus with my hearty desire of the gracious and blessed presence of God among you in all your weighty affairs, I humbly take leave and rest your servant to command in our Savour Christ,

JOHN ELIOT.

this 23d of the 8th 1648.

M.—See page 134.

The next petition is exceedingly interesting.

To the Honorable the Governor and Council sitting at Boston the 13*th of the* 6*th*, 1675.
The humble petition of John Eliot,

SHEWETH,

That the terrour of selling away such Indians in the Ilands for perpetual Slaves who shall yield up themselves to your mercy is likely to be an effectual prolongation of the warre and such an exasperation of them as may produce we know not what evil consequences upon all the land. Christ hath said, "Blessed are the merciful, for they shall obtain mercy." This [treatment] of them is worse than death. To put to death men that have deserved to die is an ordinance of God and a blessing is promised to it. It may be done in faith. The design of Christ in these last days is not to extirpate nations but to gospelize them. He will spread the Gospel sound the world about, rev. 11. 15. The kingdoms of the world have become the kingdoms of our Lord and of his Christ. His sovereign hand and grace hath brought the Gospel into these dark places of the earth. When we came we declared to the world, and it is recorded, yea we are instructed by our letters patent from the King's majesty that the endeavour of the Indians conversion not their extirpation was one great end of our enterprize in coming to these ends of the earth. The Lord hath so succeeded his work as that (by his grace) they have the Holy Scriptures and sundry of themselves able to teach their countrymen the good knowledge of God. The light of the Gospel is risen among those who sat in darkness and in the region of the shadow of death. And however some of them have refused to receive the Gospel, and are now incensed in their spirits unto a warre against the English, yet by that good promise, Ps. 1: 1—6, I doubt not but the meaning of Christ is to open the door for the free passage of the Gospel among them, and that the Lord will publish that word, v. 6. Yet have I set my king on my holy hill of Syon, though some rage at it. My humble request is if you would follow Christ his design in this matter to promote the free passage of religion among them and not destroy them. To send them away from the light of the Gospel which Christ hath graciously given them unto a place, a state, a way of spiritual darkness to the eternal ruin of their souls is as I apprehend to act contrary to the mind of Christ. God's command is that we should inlarge the kingdom of Jesus Christ. Esay, 54 : 2. Enlarge the place of thy tent. It seemeth to me that to sell them away for slaves is to hinder the inlargement of his kingdom. How can a Christian [soule yield to act]—(these words are indistinct) in casting away their soules for which Christ hath with an eminent hand provided an offer of the Gospel. To sell soules for money seemeth to me a dangerous merchandize. If they deserve to dy, it is far better to be put to death under godly [rulers] who will take care if meanes may be used that they may die penitently. To fall away from all meanes of grace when Christ hath provided meanes of grace for them, is for us to be active in the destroying their soules when we are highly obliged to seek their conversion and salvation and have opportunity in our hands so to doe. Deut. 23: 15, 16.* A fugitive servant from his Pagan master might not be delivered to his master, but be kept in Israel for the good of his soul. How much less lawful is it to sell away souls from under the light of the Gospel into a condition where their souls will be utterly lost, so far as appertains unto man. All men (of reading) condemned the Spaniard for cruelty upon this point for destroying men and depopulating the land. The country is large enough, here is land enough for them and us to, Prov. 14 : 28. In the multitude of people is the King's honor. It will be much to the glory of Christ to have many brought in to worship his great name. I beseech the honored Council to pardon my boldnesse, and let the case of conscience be discussed orderly before the thing be acted. Cover my weaknesse and weigh the reason and religion that laboreth in this great case of conscience.

---

* "Thou shalt not deliver unto his master the servant which is escaped," &c.

N.—See page 135.

The following petition of Mr. Eliot illustrates the kind interest which he took in the common and private affairs of the Indians. I have copied it from Mass. State Papers, (Indian Papers) 30. p. 15. 1639—1705.

PETITION THAT TWO INDIANS MAY HAVE THEIR DUE.

The humble petition of John Eliot to this Honorable Court.

First in the behalfe of Totherswompe unto whom one of Uncas his men doth owe 18 fathom of wampompeague for 6 beare skins and he cannot obtain justice with ease and therefore doth humbly intreat this honored Court to procure justice for him in this particular. Phoxon well knoweth his demand is just and true, as Thomas and Stanton can testify.

The other is in behalf of Anonganisch, who lost 17 fathom which Uncas and his men tooke unjustly from him 3 years since when they fell upon the Indians by Mr. Winthrop's plantation, and he saith that when his case was at this Court formerly heard The Governour promised him that he should have justice, and that doth embolden him to sue again in the case. The bringing them to doe justice doth so far cause them to honour and acknowledge God and therefore I humbly entreat your favour in furtherance of the same, and so commending all your weighty occasions to the blessing of the Lord.

Your worships servant
in Jesus Christ,
JOHN ELIOT.*

O.—See page 48.

THE CHURCH IN ROXBURY.

(See Am. Quarterly Register, Vol. 8th.)

Thomas Welde, the first Minister of Roxbury, was a minister in Essex, England. Re-

---

* Those who are interested in the subjects referred to in other petitions of Mr. Eliot may find those petitions as follows:

Petition that the Indians may have more land, Mass. State Papers, 30, page 31.

Petition in relation to exchange of land with the Indians, do. do. page 81.

Statement of John Eliot respecting lands, do. do. pp. 99, 100.

Complains of wrong done to the Nipmucks by the Narragansetts, do. do. page 138.

Gookin's and Eliot's petition for lands for the Christian Indians, do. do. p. 286.

There are also some original MSS. of Mr. Eliot's in the Hutchinson papers in the Library of the Mass. Historical Society, but they are somewhat illegible and of no special pertinency to the present work.

fusing to conform to the requirements of the Established Church, he sought the quiet enjoyment of the rights of conscience in this country. He arrived in Boston, June 5, 1632, and entered upon the pastoral office in Roxbury, at which time the Church was embodied. In 1641, he was sent as an agent, with Rev. Hugh Peters, to England for the Province and never returned.

JOHN ELIOT became teacher of the Church in Roxbury, Nov. 5, 1632. The next year he became colleague with Mr. Welde.

SAMUEL DANFORTH was colleague with Mr. Eliot after Mr. Welde went to England. He continued in office 24 years.

NEHEMIAH WALTER, born in Ireland, came to Boston at the age of 16. Graduated at Harvard College, and was the third colleague of Mr. Eliot. He had so good knowledge of the French Language that he preached to a society of French Protestants while their Pastor was absent. Whitefield called him "the good old Puritan." A well known publication of his is called, "The Wonderfulness of Christ."

THOMAS WALTER, his son, became colleague with his father, but died 7 years after.

OLIVER PEABODY, son of the Missionary at Natick of the same name, succeeded Mr. Walter, but continued only 18 months, and died when on the eve of being married, aged 27.

Amos Adams, was Pastor at Roxbury 22 years and died of the epidemic which prevailed in the camp at Roxbury and Cambridge. The title of one of his published Sermons was, The only Hope and Refuge of Sinners.

Eliphalet Porter succeeded him and continued in office 51 years.

George Putnam, the present Pastor, was ordained colleague with him, July 7, 1830.

A Church was organized in Roxbury, Sept. 18, 1834, composed of Members of Evangelical sentiments, and of the Orthodox Congregational denomination. It took the name of "Eliot Church."

Rev. John S. C. Abbott was ordained Pastor, Nov. 25, 1835.

Rev. Augustus C. Thompson was ordained Pastor, July 27, 1842.

P.—See page 51.

ROXBURY "ELIOT SCHOOL FUND."

"Eliot School Fund had its origin in the donation of Rev. John Eliot, of Roxbury, well known as the Apostle to the Indians, who, in the year 1689, conveyed an estate of about seventy-five acres of land to certain persons and their heirs, as Trustees for "the maintenance, support and encouragement of a school and school master at that part of Roxbury, commonly called Jamaica or the Pond Plain, for the teaching and instructing of the children of that end of the town (together with such Indians and negroes as shall or may come to the said school) and to no other use, intent, or purpose whatever. This is the language of the deed." (The fund was afterwards increased by donations.)

"The Eliot school fund consists (1840) of $9,699 94. The School also possesses some real estate, which yields an annual income of $381."

Report of the Committee on the School Fund, Roxbury. Auditor's Reports, 1831—1846.

The following are the principal of Mr. Eliot's publications. It is remarkable that no entire Sermon of his has been preserved.

Answer to Norcott's book against Infant Baptism.

The Harmony of the Gospels in the Holy History of Jesus Christ.

The Christian Commonwealth.

The Divine management of Gospel Churches by the Ordinance of Councils, constituted in order according to the Scriptures, which may be a means of uniting those two holy and eminent parties, the Presbyterians and the Congregational.

Indian Bible, Catechism, and Psalms of David in metre.

Baxter's "Call to the unconverted," translated into the Indian Tongue.

The Practice of Piety, translated into the Indian Tongue. This book was written by Lewis Bayly, for some time Chaplain to James the First. In 1792, it had reached the *seventy-first* edition. The author was promoted to the see of Bangor, 1616. See Lib. Am. Biog. V. 245. Francis' Life of Eliot. BIOG. BRITAN. Art. BAYLY.

Thomas Shepard's Sincere Convert, translated into the Indian tongue.

Thomas Shepard's Sound Believer, translated into the Indian tongue.

Indian Primer.

This little book has been of great help to linguists by the division of syllables in it for children, thereby giving learners of a larger growth some insight into the formation of Indian words.

NOTE.

The following appropriate conclusion to this volume came to hand just as the last pages were going to press.

THE CHOCTAWS TO THEIR WHITE BRETHREN OF IRELAND.—A meeting for the relief of the starving poor of Ireland was held at the Choctaw agency, on the 23d ult. Maj. William Armstrong was called to the chair, and J. B. Luce was appointed secretary. A circular of the "Memphis committee" was read by Maj. Armstrong, after which the meeting contributed $ 170. All subscribed, agents, missionaries, traders and Indians, a considerable portion of which fund was made up by the latter. The "poor Indian" sending his mite to the poor Irish!

[*Arkansas Intelligencer*, *April* 3.]

www.ingramcontent.com/pod-product-compliance
Lightning Source LLC
LaVergne TN
LVHW020221110826
845151LV00003B/787